Christ Our Life

2

God Cares for Us

Authors

Sisters of Notre Dame
Chardon, Ohio

Reviewers

Sister Mary Judith Bucco, S.N.D.

Sister Margaret Mary Friel, S.N.D.

Sister Mary Jean Hoelke, S.N.D.

Sister Mary Cordell Kopec, S.N.D.

Sister Mary Charlotte Manzo, S.N.D.

Sister Ann Mary McLaughlin, S.N.D.

Sister Mary Donnalee Resar, S.N.D.

Sister Katherine Mary Skrabec, S.N.D.

Sister Eileen Marie Skutt, S.N.D.

Sister Mary Jane Vovk, S.N.D.

LOYOLA PRESS.
A JESUIT MINISTRY
Chicago

Nihil Obstat
Reverend John G. Lodge, S.S.L., S.T.D.
Censor Deputatus
May 22, 2007

Imprimatur
Reverend John F. Canary, S.T.L., D.Min.
Vicar General, Archdiocese of Chicago
May 25, 2007

Christ Our Life
found to be in conformity

The Ad Hoc Committee to Oversee the Use of the Catechism, United States Conference of Catholic Bishops, has found the doctrinal content of this catechetical series, copyright 2009, to be in conformity with the *Catechism of the Catholic Church.*

The *Nihil Obstat* and *Imprimatur* are official declarations that a book is free of doctrinal and moral error. No implication is contained therein that those who have granted the *Nihil Obstat* and *Imprimatur* agree with the content, opinions, or statements expressed. Nor do they assume any legal responsibility associated with publication.

Acknowledgments

Excerpts from the *New American Bible* with Revised New Testament and Psalms Copyright © 1991, 1986, 1970 Confraternity of Christian Doctrine, Inc., Washington, DC. All rights reserved. No portion of the *New American Bible* may be reprinted without permission in writing from the copyright holder.

Excerpts from the English translation of *The Roman Missal* © 1973, International Committee on English in the Liturgy, Inc. (ICEL); excerpts from the English translation of the *Rite of Penance* © 1974, ICEL; excerpts from the English translation of *A Book of Prayers* © 1982, ICEL; excerpts from the English translation of *Book of Blessings* © 1988, ICEL. All rights reserved.

English translation of the Apostles' Creed and the Nicene Creed by the International Consultation on English Texts.

Loyola Press has made every effort to locate the copyright holders for the cited works used in this publication and to make full acknowledgment for their use. In the case of any omissions, the publisher will be pleased to make suitable acknowledgments in future editions.

Cover art: Lori Lohstoeter
Cover design: Loyola Press and Think Design Group
Interior design: Think Design Group and
Mia Basile, Loyola Press

ISBN 13: 978-0-8294-2407-2, ISBN 10: 0-8294-2407-5

© 2009 Loyola Press and
Sisters of Notre Dame, Chardon, Ohio

Dedicated to St. Julie Billiart, foundress of the Sisters of Notre Dame, in gratitude for her inspiration and example

LOYOLAPRESS.
A JESUIT MINISTRY

3441 N. Ashland Avenue
Chicago, Illinois 60657
(800) 621-1008
www.loyolapress.com

Webcrafters, Inc. / Madison, WI, USA / 04-10 / 3rd printing

Contents

Especially for Families

A Note to Families begins on page v. There is a Letter Home at the beginning of each unit. At the end of each unit you will find a Family Feature that explores ways to nurture faith at home.

Note to Families

Goals of the Program

God Cares for Us prepares your child to celebrate the Sacrament of Penance and Reconciliation and the Sacrament of the Eucharist. Throughout the year, your child will learn many signs of God's loving care and practical ways to use his or her talents to share God's love with others. The program leads the children to respond joyfully to God's call to give themselves in love to him and to others.

A Family Program

A separate Reconciliation booklet, *Jesus Gives Me His Peace,* and Mass booklet, *Jesus Gives Himself,* will help you prepare your child for the sacraments. Two family celebrations in this book are immediate preparation for your child's celebration of Reconciliation (page 82d) and First Communion (page 126d).

Each unit in this book begins with a letter home that summarizes the message to be presented in class. Each chapter highlights one aspect of the message presented each week. The Building Family Faith sections summarize the chapter's message and suggest related family activities under four topics.

Reflect Gives a scriptural reading that can be done by a parent or older child in the family.

Discuss as a Family Opens discussion about bringing our faith into daily life.

Pray Sums up the message for the week in a short prayer of the heart, which all can say daily. This prayer might be copied and posted on the refrigerator or a mirror or added to meal prayers or other family prayers.

Do Provides ideas for sharing at meals, playing games, and enjoying family activities related to the message of the chapter. Storybooks available in public libraries are sometimes suggested.

Review with your child the text and booklet pages covered in class. Each unit ends with Family Feature pages that suggest a family custom and provide review activities.

Note to Families

Ten Principles to Nurture Your Child's Faith

1. Listen with your heart as well as with your head.

2. Encourage wonder and curiosity in your child.

3. Coach your child in empathy early. It's a building block for morality.

4. Display religious artwork in your home. This will serve as a steady witness that faith is an important part of life.

5. Gently guide your child to a life of honesty.

6. Whenever appropriate, model for your child how to say "I'm sorry."

7. Eat meals together regularly as a family. It will be an anchor for your child in days to come.

8. Pray together in good times and bad. Worship regularly together as a family.

9. Be generous to those who need help. Make helping others an important focus of your life as a family.

10. See your child for the wonder that God made. Communicate your conviction that your child was created for a noble purpose—to serve God and others in this life and to be happy with God forever in the next.

Visit **www.ChristOurLife.org/family** for more family resources.

God Gives Us Life and Love

I praise you, so wonderfully you made me; wonderful are your works!

Psalm 139:14

A Letter Home

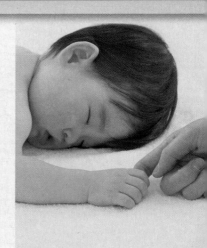

Dear Parents and Family,

Welcome to Christ Our Life! You have the opportunity to be involved in your child's learning about the Catholic faith. Your interest, participation, and discussions at home will expand your child's understanding of these lessons and convey a message about their importance.

This first unit of Christ Our Life introduces your child to an all-loving God who cares personally about each of us. Your child will learn that everything and everyone are gifts from God and be led to a greater awareness of God's presence in the everyday.

In the second chapter, the children learn that God's greatest gift is his Son, Jesus, who freed us from sin. Jesus shows us how we can enjoy life with God forever.

The children will be offered a deeper understanding of Baptism and the Church in Chapter Three. Baptism is an initiation into a new life united with the Father, the Son, and the Holy Spirit. This leads to a discussion of a key mystery of our faith, the Trinity.

Baptism also joins us to the Church. The children will learn how the Church shares and teaches God's Word, celebrates his presence among us, and is dedicated to living in his love.

At the end of three of the chapters in this unit, the children will bring home a review of the chapter along with the "Building Family Faith" feature. This feature gives you a quick review of what your child learned and offers practical ways to reinforce the lesson at home so that the whole family may benefit. At the end of the fourth chapter, the review for this unit, the children will bring home a Family Feature handout to help nurture the family's faith at home.

Visit **www.ChristOurLife.org/family** for more family resources.

God Is the Giver of Gifts

God's Gifts Show His Love

God is the GIVER OF GIFTS.
God gives the gift of summer.
I feel the warm sun on my back
and cool blades of grass beneath my feet.
And I know that GOD IS GOOD!

God sends the gifts of rain, colorful flowers,
trees to climb, and lakes with waves.
I know the gift of the touch of a soft,
furry kitten and the sight of a puppy's wagging tail.
And I know that GOD IS GOOD!

God gives the gift of people who love me
and care for me when I fall and scrape my knee,
who help me with my school work,
who hug me when I feel sad or lonely or scared.
And I know that GOD LOVES ME!

We Are Gifts

God made everything. He made the sun and the moon. He made plants and animals. All creation is a gift from God. God is Father, Son, and Holy Spirit. We call this the **Trinity**.

God made us. We are gifts too. God made us like himself. We can think. We can choose.
We can love.

Gifts are to be given. We give ourselves to others. We give ourselves to God.

I give you thanks for making me so wonderful.

adapted from Psalm 139:14

God Gives Us Gifts

God gives us a mind so that we can think.

Print one thing you learned last year.

titanic

We can choose, too.

Choose the pet you like best. Make a circle around it.

God has also given us a heart to **love** with.

Whom do you love in a special way?

Write their names or draw their pictures in the heart.

Asher

God Cares for His Gifts

One day Jesus said,

> "God loves you more than the birds. He loves you more than the flowers. God takes good care of you."

adapted from Luke 12:24–29

Trace the bird and the flowers. Color them.

A Moment with Jesus

Think about the wonderful things God made. Tell Jesus how you will help care for God's gift of creation. Listen to Jesus tell you how much God loves and cares for you.

God's Gift is Special

To Thomas
From GOD

Pick a gift of God that is special to you.

Draw the gift in the gift box above. Print your name on the tag.

Was it hard to choose just one gift? God is good to give us so many gifts. What would you like to say to God when you think about God's gifts to you?

Print it here:

Thanks you God.

Each Person Is a Special Gift

God made everybody. God loves everybody, too.

Circle each person God made and loves.

We Remember

How did God make us?

God made us in the image and likeness of himself. We can think, choose, and love.

What is the Trinity?

The Trinity is God. God is Father, Son, and Holy Spirit.

Word to Know

Trinity

We Respond

How wonderful are your gifts. They are more than I can count.

adapted from Psalm 40:6

Building Family Faith

ALL CREATION speaks of God's love, beauty, and goodness, but human beings have a special relationship with God. Each one of us is made in the image of God, and we are called to do our part to take proper care of the world God has entrusted to us.

REFLECT

"Notice the ravens: they do not sow or reap; they have neither storehouse nor barn, yet God feeds them. How much more important are you than birds!" (Luke 12:24)

DISCUSS AS A FAMILY

• How has God taken care of you in your life?

• What are some typical ways that people take care of one another in our family?

Visit **www.ChristOurLife.org/family** for more family resources.

PRAY

Thank you, Lord, for all your gifts.

DO

• At family mealtimes this week, ask each person to tell one thing he or she is grateful for.

• Show gratitude for creation by picking up litter.

• Help your child see that everyone is created in the image of God by performing a kind act, such as offering to help a neighbor with a chore.

• Read a story or poem that evokes an appreciation for nature.

Jesus Is God's Best Gift

Jesus Shows Us the Father's Love

Maria was playing in the ocean. A big wave knocked her down. Under the water Maria could not breathe. She could not cry for help. She did not know how to swim. She was so scared.

Then Maria felt someone lift her up. She was pulled out of the water. She could see the sun again. Her big brother had saved her life.

Jesus came to save us. He was sent by the Father. Jesus is God's best gift to us. He tells us about God. He teaches us how to live.

Most wonderful of all, Jesus gives us new life. We call this new life grace.

Jesus Saves Us

Jesus once told a story about a seed. He said,

> "It must die. If it dies, it brings forth much fruit."

adapted from John 12:24

Jesus suffered and died on the cross. Then he rose from the dead with new life. He shares this new life with us. Jesus died for our sins so that we could live forever. We can go to heaven. Jesus is our Savior.

The Story of a Seed

Trace the dotted lines. Color the pictures.

1  When you plant a seed, it dies.

2  It grows into a new plant.

3 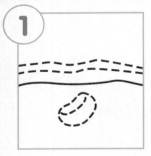 Flowers grow.

4 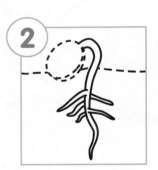 Fruit grows.

The Friends of Jesus Are the Church

Jesus called people to be his friends. He called Peter, Andrew, James, and John from their boats. "Follow me," Jesus invited. These friends became his **disciples**, his Church.

Mary, the Mother of God, is the Mother of the Church. Everyone in the Church tries to live and love like Jesus. The Holy Spirit guides the Church.

Jesus calls you to be his friend. You are a disciple too. This means you follow Jesus. You are a member of his Church. You share the life of Jesus and try to live as he did.

Jesus Shares His Life with Us

Jesus told us about our life with him.

He said,

> "I am the vine, you are the branches. A branch cannot bear fruit if it is cut off from the vine. If you live in me, you can do many good things."

adapted from John 15:5–7

Jesus is the vine. We are the branches. Our good deeds are the fruit.

Color the vine and the branches. Then draw in fruit. Next to each piece of fruit, write a good deed you can do.

We Pray the Sign of the Cross

We remember Jesus' love. We remember that Jesus saved us.
We make the Sign of the Cross.

1 In the name of the Father,

2 and of the Son,

3 and of the Holy

4 Spirit.

5 Amen.

Where is your hand when you say these words?

Write the correct number next to each picture.

A Moment with Jesus

Every cross reminds us that Jesus died for us. Thank Jesus for loving us so much. Tell Jesus how much you love him.

We Remember

How did Jesus show us the Father's love?

Jesus died and rose from the dead. He brought us new life.

What did Jesus say about our life and his?

Jesus said,

"I am the vine, you are the branches. A branch cannot bear fruit if it is cut off from the vine. If you live in me, you can do many good things."

adapted from John 15:5–7

Word to Know

disciple

We Respond

Thank you, God Our Father, for your best gift, Jesus.

Building Family Faith

GOD SHOWS HIS LOVE for the human family by giving us his Son, Jesus. Jesus died and rose to save us. He shows us how we can be happy every day and live with God forever.

REFLECT

Jesus said to him, "I am the way and the truth and the life." John 14:6

DISCUSS AS A FAMILY

- How do we come to know God better by listening to Jesus' words?
- Discuss how it feels to be lost and how good it is to find the way again.

PRAY

Lord, I'm listening. Help me hear your Word.

DO

- At family mealtimes, have your child slowly make the Sign of the Cross and lead grace.
- Take a nature walk and view how new life emerges from death.
- Read *The Parables of Jesus* by Tomie dePaola (Holiday House, 1995).

Visit **www.ChristOurLife.org/family** for more family resources.

Jesus Lives in His Church

God Gives New Life in Baptism

Think of how God loves us. He calls us his children and that is what we are.

adapted from 1 John 3:1

Jesus gave us grace at our Baptism. He took away **original sin.** Original sin is the result of the sin of Adam and Eve. At Baptism, the Holy Spirit came to live in us. We became God's children. We became members of God's family, the Church.

Baptism is a **sacrament.** A sacrament is a way that the Church meets Jesus. It is a special celebration of God's family. At Baptism we received the gift of **faith**. Faith helps us believe in God. **Confirmation** is a sacrament that helps us live like children of God.

The Church Welcomed Us in Baptism

Here are pictures of Molly Elizabeth's Baptism from the Graham family photo album.

Father Ron greets Molly, saying, "The Christian family welcomes you with great joy." Molly's parents and he make the Sign of the Cross over her.

1

Father Ron reads from the Bible. Then he and everyone in the church pray, "Give this child the new life of Baptism."

The parents and godparents promise to help Molly live like a good Christian.

2

3

Father Ron baptizes Molly. He pours water on her head. He says, "Molly Elizabeth, I baptize you in the name of the Father, and of the Son, and of the Holy Spirit."

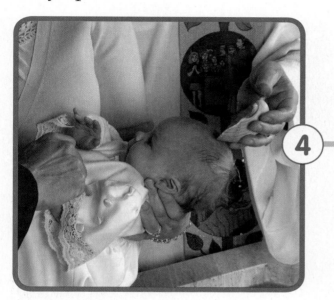

4

Father Ron lays a white robe on Molly. He says, "You have clothed yourself in Christ."

5

6

A candle is lit. Father Ron says, "Receive the light of Christ."

The family and friends are filled with joy.

They celebrate Molly's new life.

We Belong to the Church

People who believe in Jesus are a community of love. They are called Christians. They worship God. They try to love others as Jesus did. They are God's people, the Church. You belong to the Catholic Church. It is a part of God's people.

Jesus Helps Us Through His Church

The risen Jesus is still present in his Church. He is the head of his Church. He sent the Holy Spirit to help us.

Jesus gave leaders to his Church. They help us grow in God's life. They lead us to the Father. The twelve apostles were the first leaders of the Church.

The leaders today are the pope and **bishops. Priests** help the bishops serve the Church. We help one another to build up the Church. We use the gifts God has given us.

You Are a Part of the Church

You are no longer strangers or visitors. You belong to the saints and are part of God's people.

adapted from Ephesians 2:19

Add yourself to this picture of the Church.

A Moment with Jesus

Imagine yourself with all the people in the picture of the Church. Think quietly of everything Jesus does for you through the Church. Tell Jesus one thing you will do today to help his Church. Thank him for calling you to be a part of his Church.

Print the name of the pope in the first box. Print the name of your pastor in the middle box. Then print your name in the last box. Everyone is important in the Church.

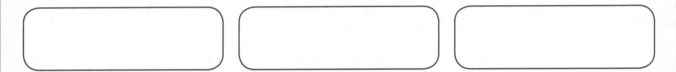

We Remember

What did Jesus give us when we were baptized?

Jesus gave us a share in his life.

What is a Christian?

A Christian is a person who believes in Jesus. A Christian tries to love as Jesus did. Many Christians belong to the Catholic Church.

Words to Know

bishop   Confirmation
faith   original sin
priest   sacrament

We Respond

Father, help us share our gifts with others to build up the Church.

Building Family Faith

BAPTISM WELCOMES US into the family of Christ. As Christians, we are called to live in love, united with all the People of God, under the spiritual leadership of the pope and the bishops.

REFLECT

In this way the love of God was revealed to us: God sent his only Son into the world so that we might have life through him. (1 John 4:9)

DISCUSS AS A FAMILY

• how sharing and giving are signs of our love for God and others.

• why you brought your child to be baptized.

• how the Church helps us live in love.

PRAY

Dear Jesus, help me grow in faith, hope, and love.

DO

• At family mealtimes this week, talk about the godparents of each family member and why they were chosen.

• Select a special candle to place on the dinner table and talk about how light sustains us physically and spiritually.

• Read a story about welcoming others: *Mr. Popper's Penguins* by Richard Atwater (Little, Brown, 1938) or *Always Room for One More* by Sorche Nic Leodhas (Henry Holt, 1965).

Visit **www.ChristOurLife.org/family** for more family resources.

God Speaks to Us

Jesus Helps Us Hear God Speak

Jesus came to visit a little town. Some people brought a deaf man to him. The man could not hear or speak. The people asked Jesus to help him. Jesus touched the man's ears and mouth and said, "Be opened." At once the man could hear and speak. All the people said, "Jesus has done good things."

adapted from Mark 7:31–37

Jesus helped the man hear and speak. The man was amazed at what he heard. He was surprised he could speak.

What is your favorite sound to hear? God's word

Who is your favorite person to talk to?  brothers

Our Hearts Are Opened to God's Call

In Baptism, God opened our hearts to hear him. He speaks to us every day. God calls us to him in everything he created.

God speaks to us in the Bible. The **Old Testament** tells us about God's plan for all people. The **New Testament** tells the story of Jesus and the early Church.

God speaks to us through Jesus. Jesus came to show us the Father's love. He wants us to speak to others about God.

Saints are people who heard God speaking to them too. They chose to serve God in a special way. Some saints served him by caring for other people. All the saints now live with God in heaven.

Right: Saint Juan Diego
Below: Saint Thérèse of Lisieux

Church Puzzle

Use the words in the candle and the clues below for the puzzles in the church windows. Then draw a flame for the candle.

Top Puzzle

1. another name for Jesus
2. the Mother of the Church
3. a community that believes in Jesus

Left Puzzle

1. leaders of the Church
2. _____ showed the Church how to live.

3. We try to _____ as Jesus did.

Right Puzzle

1. someone who tries to live like Jesus
2. God shared his _____ with us at Baptism.
3. We became God's children at _____.

Christians Use Their Gifts for God

When John Bosco was a boy, he learned how to juggle and do other tricks.

John used these gifts to spread God's love. After his friends said their prayers or took part in Mass, he would do some tricks for them.

Later John became a priest. He started a home and a school for boys. John showed the boys how to love God and use their gifts for him. Now John is a saint. We call him Saint John Bosco.

God has given gifts to everyone. We can use our gifts to help people love God and to help make the world a better place.

Words to Know

New Testament   Old Testament saint

We Remember

How does God speak to us?
God speaks to us in the Bible and through Jesus.

We Respond

Lord Jesus, help us learn from you how to live good lives.

The Vine and the Branches

Leader: Let us praise and bless the Lord, who gave us new life in Baptism. Praise be to God now and forever.

All: Praise be to God now and forever.

Leader: Let us listen to some words of Jesus from the Gospel of John.

Reader: One day Jesus said to his disciples,

"I am the vine and you are the branches. You must live in me as I live in you. A branch cannot bear fruit if it is cut off from the vine. If you live in me, you can do many good things."

(adapted from John 15:5–7)

The Gospel of the Lord.

All: Praise to you,
Lord Jesus Christ.

Leader: God gave us new life at our Baptism and made us members of his Church. In Baptism we use water to remind us of the grace we receive in this sacrament. Let us each bless ourselves with this water while thanking God. In the name of the Father, and of the Son, and of the Holy Spirit.

Amen.

Leader: We are joined to one another and to all members of the Church. Let us ask some of the saints to pray to God for us.

Leader: Holy Mary, Mother of God

All: Pray for us.

Leader: Saint Joseph

All: Pray for us.

Leader: Saint Peter

All: Pray for us.

Leader: Saint John Bosco

All: Pray for us.

Leader: All holy men and women

All: Pray for us.

Leader: May God keep us close to him and to one another in Jesus. And may we continue to do good things with the help of the Holy Spirit. We ask this in Jesus' name.

All: Amen.

Family Feature

Initiation and Invitation

Few of us recall our other birth day—our Baptism, the day we were born into a life in Christ. Most of us don't eat cake or open gifts to mark the occasion; in fact, there's a fair chance we don't even know the date of our Baptism.

But it was a significant day that touched off a series of events. It was a fresh start without original sin. It was an initiation into the life of grace and life within the Church.

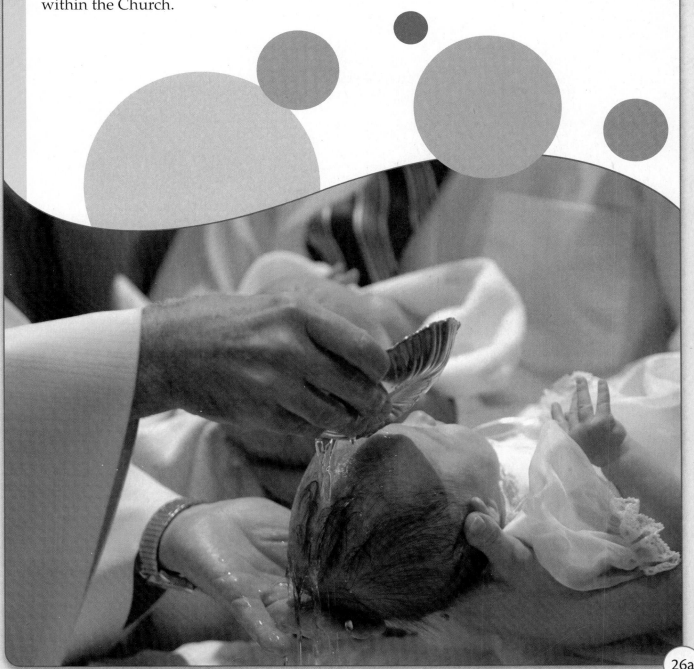

Family Feature

The steps in the ritual for the Sacrament of Baptism, including the pouring of water and the lighting of a candle, give us a tangible way to experience God's welcome and our new life. As our Creator, God knows his love and forgiveness are beyond our imagining, so he works through the sacraments. The ritual of the sacraments affords us the opportunity to stop, to contemplate, and to celebrate God's loving gifts.

Consider what the symbols of the Sacrament of Initiation mean. Think of what water provides for us daily. It sustains life and cleanses our bodies. In the Sacrament of Baptism, water symbolizes our freedom from original sin and our new life in God. The light of the candle reminds us that we are to bring the light of Christ into the world.

Through the sacraments, we are graced with God's life. And it all begins with our Baptism, a day often forgotten after the initial celebration but a day that ought to be remembered and celebrated yearly.

A Re-Birthday Party

Celebrate a re-birthday! Purchase one floating candle for every member of your family. Gather everyone around the table, fill a shallow baking dish or glass bowl with water, float the candles on the surface, and light them.

Begin with the Sign of the Cross—a sign of our salvation. Follow by choosing a person to read this statement of our beliefs as members of the Church:

I believe in God, the Father almighty,

creator of heaven and earth.

I believe in Jesus Christ, his only Son, our Lord.

He was conceived by the power of the Holy Spirit

and born of the Virgin Mary.

He suffered under Pontius Pilate,

was crucified, died, and was buried.

He descended to the dead.

On the third day he arose again.

He ascended into heaven,

and is seated at the right hand of the Father.

He will come again to judge the living and the dead.

I believe in the Holy Spirit,

the holy catholic Church,

the communion of saints,

the forgiveness of sins,

the resurrection of the body,

and the life everlasting.

Amen.

Repeat the Sign of the Cross. Then share a re-birthday cake—preferably white, to recall the white gown or robe you each wore at Baptism.

Plan for future re-birthday parties by repeating the ceremony on the date of each family member's Baptism.

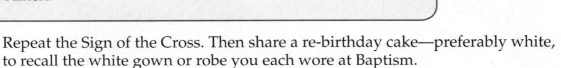

Family Feature

Let's Not Forget

Create a calendar of sacramental firsts for the children in your family. On the calendar, mark the date and note the year of each child's first celebration of each sacrament. The calendar will serve as a journal of the child's spiritual journey as well as a reminder of the importance of these first celebrations.

Glad for Godparents

Each year, on the date of a family member's Baptism, send a card to his or her godparents, thanking them for their support in the faith. Offer a prayer for those godparents and for godparents everywhere, that they may be guided by the Holy Spirit as they guide others.

If possible, you might even invite them to their godchild's re-birthday celebration.

A Warm Welcome

Donate a children's Bible or prayer book to your parish, to be given to a newly baptized child. Consider organizing such donations as a ministry, welcoming new members to the faith.

Visit **www.ChristOurLife.org/family** for more family resources.

Jesus Calls Us to Give Ourselves in Love

God is love, and whoever remains in love remains in God and God in him.

1 John 4:16

A Letter Home

Dear Parents and Family,

This is a special year in your child's faith development. Preparation for the Sacrament of Reconciliation will offer an opportunity to introduce new concepts and develop your child's relationship with God in exciting new ways.

As part of this preparation, Unit Two introduces the children to the Ten Commandments. They will discover how the first three commandments ask us to express our love for God as Jesus did: by praying to God, by speaking of him with love, and by keeping the Sabbath holy. The unit continues with discussions of the remaining seven commandments, which focus on loving others as Jesus does.

The children are presented with the simple ideas in each commandment, learning that they are to pray (1st Commandment), to honor God's name (2nd Commandment), to keep the Sabbath (3rd Commandment), to obey (4th Commandment), to be kind (5th Commandment), to be respectful (6th and 9th Commandments), to be honest (7th and 10th Commandments), and to be truthful (8th Commandment).

The Ten Commandments are available online at www. ChristOurLife.org, under Catholic Traditions within the Resources section. Being mindful of how the Ten Commandments are lived out in your home will help make these loving directions from God seem real for your child.

At the end of three of the chapters in this unit, the children will bring home a review of the chapter along with the "Building Family Faith" feature. At the end of the unit, the children will bring home a Family Feature to help nurture the family's faith at home.

Visit **www.ChristOurLife.org/family** for more family resources.

Jesus Shows Us How to Love God Our Father

Jesus Loved God His Father

We like to celebrate. God made us to celebrate his love. He made us to love and be joyful.

Jesus said:

"Live in my love. Keep my commandments. Then my joy will be in you, and your joy will be full."

adapted from John 15:10–11

God gave us the **Ten Commandments.** They are rules that help us live as his children. When we follow God's rules, we are happy.

29

Jesus Pleased His Father

Jesus loved his Father very much.
He always did what pleased
his Father.

Jesus loved talking to him.
He heard his Father speaking
to him in everything.

Jesus spoke about his Father with love.

He celebrated the **Lord's Day**.

Jesus told us,

> "Love the Lord your God
> with all your heart."

adapted from Mark 12:30

Christians celebrate God's love always and
everywhere. Celebrating and loving God make us happy.

We Celebrate God's Love

Catholics celebrate God's love together at Sunday Mass.
Sunday is the Lord's Day. It is a day of rest from hard work.

Print the missing words from the hearts.

God's law in the Bible tells how to love him. We show God love

when we _pray_,

say his _name_ with love,

and celebrate the _Lord's Day_.

When we do this, we are following God's rules.
We are obeying the first three **commandments**.

We Can Pray to God Every Day

Lord, you know me so well. You know
    everything I do.
You know when I sit and when I stand.
You read my thoughts from far away.
When I work and when I rest, you watch
    over me.
There is nothing I say that you do not
    know.
You are all around me, saving me with
    your hand.

adapted from Psalm 139:1–5

Add yourself to the picture.

Make yourself as colorful as
the rest of God's creation.

A Moment with Jesus

Remember Jesus is with us every
second of every minute of every day. Sit
quietly and enjoy being with Jesus.

Make word banners. Fill in the missing words by using the clues at the bottom of the page.

Across

1. We p r a y when we talk and listen to God.
3. The Lord's Day is S u n d a y.
6. When we keep God's commandments, we have j o y in our hearts.
7. We take part in M _____ to celebrate the Lord's Day.

Down

2. Sunday is a day to r e s t from hard work.
4. We honor God's n a m e.
5. We l i v e God with our whole heart.
8. We s _____ and pray in church.

Work the puzzle. Use this code.

e	h	r	v	w	y
1	2	3	4	5	6

God is

e v e r y w h e r e .
1 4 1 3 6 5 2 1 3 1

We Remember

What is God's law?

"Love the Lord your God with all your heart and soul."

How do we live this way?

We live this way by praying, saying God's name with love, and celebrating the Lord's Day.

Words to Know

commandments   Lord's Day
Ten Commandments

We Respond

Loving God, help me to show my love for you in all I do and say.

Building Family Faith

GOD SATISFIES our deepest longings. Jesus shows us how to call on God in times of joy or sorrow. We show our gratitude for God's love by gathering in prayer as a family and a Christian community.

REFLECT

Be filled with the Spirit, addressing one another in psalms and hymns and spiritual songs.
(Ephesians 5:18–19)

DISCUSS AS A FAMILY

• How is praying a form of talking to God? There are different types of prayers, including praise, thanksgiving, and petition.

• What are your favorite childhood memories of Sunday Mass and your family rituals associated with it?

PRAY

Dear Jesus, here's what happened today . . .

DO

• Have your child choose daily prayers to say each morning, afternoon, and evening: Hail Mary, Bless Us O Lord, Our Father.

• Plan a way to make each Sunday special by developing rituals around the Mass: cook a special breakfast before Mass or invite different friends or relatives to come to church with you each week.

• At mealtime show how songs can be a form of praise by singing a favorite Church hymn or Christmas carol.

Visit **www.ChristOurLife.org/family** for more family resources.

Jesus Shows Us How to Love Others

Jesus Gave Us the Law of Love

Jesus said,

"You shall love the Lord your God with all your heart, with all your soul, with all your mind, and with all your strength."

(Mark 12:30)

"You shall love your neighbor as yourself."

(Mark 12:31)

We call these two rules the **Great Commandment**.

Jesus went to Peter and Andrew's house with James and John. Peter's mother-in-law was sick. She was in bed with a fever. Jesus went to her and took her by the hand. The fever went away! Then Peter's mother-in-law got up and waited on Jesus and the others.

Jesus Shows Us How to Follow the Law of Love

Jesus followed God's law in the Bible. This law shows us how to love others.

  Be kind.  Be respectful.  Be honest.

Obey.

Be truthful.

Match the pictures with the words of Jesus. Put the right number in the boxes.

I will remember Jesus' words:

1. I was thirsty and you gave me drink.
2. I was hungry and you gave me food.
3. I was sick and you visited me.
4. I was a stranger and you made me welcome.

adapted from Matthew 25:35–36

Share some ways you can show that you remember Jesus' words.

We Obey When We Listen to God Our Father

Jesus said,

"I always do the things that please my Father."

adapted from John 14:31

Mary and Joseph took Jesus to Jerusalem. On the way home Mary noticed Jesus was not with them. After three days of looking for him Mary and Joseph found him in the Temple. He was talking to the teachers. Jesus was doing God his Father's work.

Jesus went home to Nazareth with Mary and Joseph. He listened to God his Father. He obeyed Mary and Joseph.

We listen to God our Father when we obey our parents. We also follow the Fourth Commandment when we do this.

Color the picture that tells the story of Jesus in the Temple.

obey

A Moment with Jesus

Think about the story of Jesus obeying Mary and Joseph. Tell Jesus about times when it is hard for you to obey your parents. Ask Jesus to help you.

Ways to Obey

Complete the sentences under the pictures with the words in the boxes.

work   come   help   pray

I will do things that please Jesus.

I will _help_ others.

I will _pray_ to God.

I will _work_ hard at school.

I will _come_ when called.

We Act in Loving Ways

Check the boxes that show someone acting in a loving manner.

What can you turn each day into?

Write the letter in the box that comes before each letter under it.

d		k	i	n	d	n	e	s	s		d	a	y
B		**L**	**J**	**O**	**E**	**O**	**F**	**T**	**T**		**E**	**B**	**Z**

We Remember

What is the Great Commandment of Jesus?

The Great Commandment of Jesus is to love God above all and to love our neighbor as ourselves.

Word to Know

Great Commandment

We Respond

Jesus, help me be loving. Help me obey those who take care of me.

Building Family Faith

JESUS INVITES US to love others as he loves us. We love as Jesus does by being kind, helpful, thoughtful, and obedient. Jesus says whatever we do to others, we do to him.

REFLECT
"For I was hungry and you gave me food, thirsty and you gave me drink."
(adapted from Matthew 25:35–40)

DISCUSS AS A FAMILY
• What do members of your family do to show you really care for one another?
• How can your family support parish and community efforts to help those in need?

PRAY
I offer you all that I am and all that I have, O Lord!

DO
• Read about or discuss incidents that show how the saints used their gifts to help others.
• Together make a sign that says, "When you are kind to others, you are kind to me." Post it in your home by a picture of Jesus or a crucifix.
• Follow a story in the news about people who are in need. Find a way to help them with prayers and donation of time or money.
• As you say grace before meals, have each person tell about one person he or she helped during the day.

Visit **www.ChristOurLife.org/family** for more family resources.

CHAPTER 7

We Give Love to Others

We Love When We Show We Are Grateful

Everything God made is good. Everything is a gift of love from God. We treat God's gifts carefully. We use them as God meant them to be used. We show we are grateful for our gifts. We live in God's love. We are full of joy.

kind

We Love When We Are Kind

Every person is a gift from God. Everyone is loved by God as his child. Everyone is important. You are important too. The Fifth Commandment tells us to show respect for others by caring for them. We care in a special way for those who are poor or sick. We also show love and respect for people when we are polite and kind.

We Love When We Show Respect

Our bodies are made by God. They are holy. The Sixth Commandment tells us to respect our bodies and the bodies of others. In marriage, husbands and wives show each other this same respect.

We Love When We Are Honest

God gave all of us earth's gifts. We are honest and obey the Seventh Commandment when we respect other people's things. We do not take them. We are careful when we use them.

We obey the Tenth Commandment when we are happy for what others have.

We Love When We Are Truthful

The Eighth Commandment tells us to tell the truth. We show that we love God and others when we are truthful. God wants us to tell the truth, even when it is hard.

A Moment with Jesus

Think of the words in the hearts. Tell Jesus which is hardest for you to be. Ask for his help. Jesus always answers your prayers.

Which commandment is being obeyed?
Write the correct number in the space provided.

5th Commandment—being kind

6th Commandment—being respectful

7th Commandment—being honest

8th Commandment—being truthful

⑧ Lucy tells her sister that she can't find the markers she borrowed.

⑤ Michael brings a glass of water to his mom, who is sick.

⑦ Maria gives her dad the dollar that fell out of his pocket.

⑦ Ann pays for the candy she wants at the store.

⑥ José returns the game his friend forgot.

⑧ Leo tells his mother that he spilled juice on the rug.

⑥ Jimmy turns off TV shows that don't show respect for our bodies.

Each balloon represents a commandment.

Choose a word from the hearts in this chapter and write it on the correct balloon.

5 I am *kind*

6 I am *respectful*

7 I am *honest*

8 I am *truthful*

We Remember

What did Jesus say about anyone who loves?

Jesus said,

"God is love, and whoever remains in love remains in God and God in him."

(1 John 4:16)

We Respond

Dear Jesus, help me

● respect your gifts and take care of them.

● be kind and caring.

● be honest and truthful.

Building Family Faith

WE FOLLOW CHRIST'S way of love when we are respectful, honest, and truthful. Jesus helps us see what is good and true when we pray.

REFLECT

"Love one another with the affection of brothers. Anticipate each other in showing respect."
(adapted from Romans 12:9–18)

DISCUSS AS A FAMILY

• What are some ways we show respect to other people? our teachers? one another in the family?

• Why is it important to tell the truth?

• How do you respect your possessions? Why is it important to take care of the good things you have in life?

PRAY

I thank you, Lord, for all I am and have.

DO

• When a family member is kind, helpful, honest, or truthful, encourage that person by saying how proud you are of him or her.

• At bedtime each night, be sure to tell your child you love him or her. This encourages your child to express affection.

• Help your child decorate a card to send to a sick or distant friend or relative.

Visit **www.ChristOurLife.org/family** for more family resources.

Jesus Calls Us to Live in Love

Saint Thérèse Made Sacrifices for Others

Thérèse was a young girl who loved God very much. She gave the gift of herself to Jesus. Jesus gave himself to her in Holy Communion.

Every day Thérèse did the things that pleased God. She made sacrifices for people who did not know God.

Thérèse asked Jesus to help her and all people love him more.

Saint Thérèse, Little Flower of Jesus, pray for us.

We Can Follow the Example of Jesus

Fill in the blanks to show some ways you can be like Jesus.

I can l i s t e n to my parents. *liten*

I can c l e a n my room. *clean*

I can s h a r e my snack with my friends.

I can p r a y to God each day.

I can f e e d my fish. *feed*

I can c l e a r the dishes from the table after supper.

I can o b e y the commandments.

I can l e a r n about God.

I can v i s i t a sick friend.

I can s m i l e at all I meet.

Use the letters in green to tell what the Little Flower of Jesus made for people who didn't know God.

S a c r i f i c e s

Word Bank

clean	clear
feed	learn
listen	obey
pray	share
smile	visit

God Calls Us to Give Ourselves

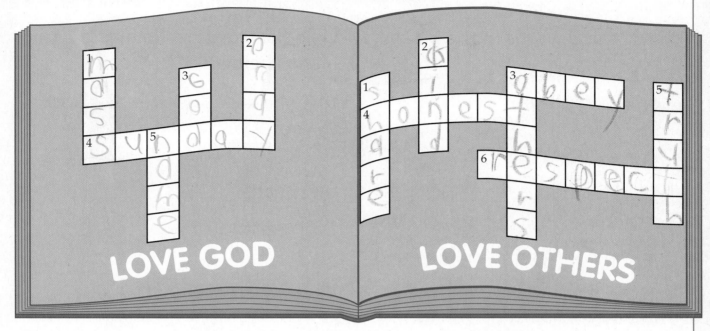

LOVE GOD

LOVE OTHERS

Read the clues. Print the answers in the puzzles above.

Word Bank name obey God share Mass respect
Sunday kind pray honest truth others

Across
4. Christians celebrate God's day on _____.

Down
1. Catholics celebrate God's day by taking part in _____.
2. We talk to God when we _____.
3. The Great Commandment tells us to love _____.
5. When we pray, we use God's holy _____.

Across
3. When we do what God wants, we _____.
4. When we take only things that belong to us, we are _____.
6. When we are polite to others, we show _____.

Down
1. When we give to others, we _____.
2. When we help others, we are _____.
3. God's Great Commandment tells us to also love _____.
5. When we say what really happened, we tell the _____.

Find these words in the puzzle.

God   love   another
Lord   heart

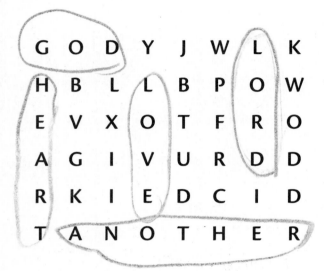

G O D Y J W L K
H B L L B P O W
E V X O T F R O
A G I V U R D D
R K I E D C I D
T A N O T H E R

Use the words to fill in the blanks below.

Love the ___Lord___ your ___God___ with all your ___Heart___.

(adapted from Mark 12:30)

Love one ___another___ as I ___love___ you.

(John 15:12)

We Remember

What are sacrifices?
  Sacrifices are acts we do to show we love God.

We Respond

Jesus, help me be a kind and loving person.

Called to Follow Jesus

Leader: In the name of the Father, and of the Son, and of the Holy Spirit. Amen.

Leader: God has called us each by name.

All: Let us bless the Lord.

Leader: This is a story from the Gospel written by Matthew.

All: Glory to you, O Lord.

Leader: Jesus was walking along when he saw a tax collector named Matthew. Matthew was sitting behind his table of money by the side of the road. When Jesus looked at Matthew, he looked deep into his heart and loved him. Then Jesus said, "Follow me." And Matthew got up and followed Jesus.

(adapted from Matthew 9:9)

The Gospel of the Lord.

All: Praise to you, Lord Jesus Christ.

49

Leader: Jesus asks you to follow him by loving God our Father.

All: We will pray to him, keep his name holy, and celebrate his day.

Leader: Jesus asks you to follow him by loving others as he loves you.

All: We will obey, be kind, share, be respectful, be honest, and tell the truth.

Leader: You have been called to follow Jesus in Baptism. In Holy Communion you will share in his life. Let us pray together in the words Jesus taught us.

All: Our Father, . . .

Family Feature

God's Ten Laws of Love

The Eisenbergs are a Jewish family. Thirteen-year-old Aaron has just celebrated his Bar Mitzvah. This means "son of the commandment." Aaron's Bar Mitzvah marks his willingness to live by the law of God.

Jewish people treasure God's laws. In their synagogues and temples the books of the Bible, including those that contain the Law, or commandments, are kept in an ark, or cabinet. This ark has a place of honor and a light burning before it just as the tabernacles in our churches have.

Family Feature

In Scripture, after giving Moses the Ten Commandments, God said,

> *"Take to heart these words. Drill them into your children.*
> *Bind them at your wrists as a sign and let them be as a pendant*
> *on your forehead. Write them on the doorposts of your houses."*

(adapted from Deuteronomy 6:6–9)

From the time of his Bar Mitzvah, whenever Aaron prays, he may wear phylacteries just as his father and other Jewish men do. These are boxes that contain Deuteronomy 6:4–9 and other Scripture passages. They are tied with leather straps to the left arm and to the forehead.

On the front doorpost of the Eisenberg home is a small box called a mezuzah, which means "doorpost." In it too is a parchment with words of God from Deuteronomy. The mezuzah reminds the Eisenbergs of God's law and how they are to observe it both at home and in the world.

Christians also embrace the Ten Commandments as a gift from God, who wants us to know the happiness of being free from sin. Jesus said he didn't come to do away with the Law. In fact, he himself followed the Law in his lifetime. He showed that the heart of the Law is to love God and love one another with a selfless love.

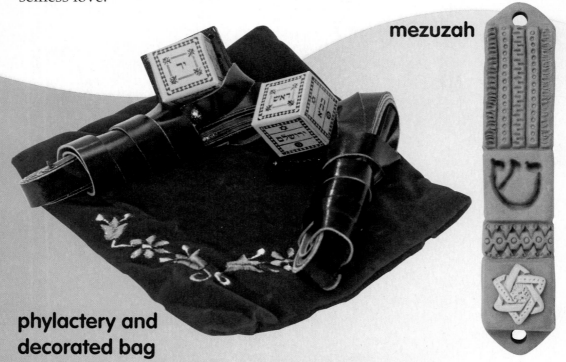

mezuzah

phylactery and decorated bag

Celebrating God's Law

Because your child has just studied the Ten Commandments, your family might plan a day to celebrate God's law, incorporating some of the following ideas:

1. Enjoy making and eating tablet-shaped cookies.

2. As a family project, shape dough to form two tablets. With a toothpick carve into them the Roman numerals from one through ten. Allow the tablets to harden, or bake them. Paint them and spray them with acrylic. Then display the tablets in your home.

3. Pray together parts of Psalm 119, which is a hymn praising God's law.

4. Watch the DVD or video *The Ten Commandments.*

5. Have one person hide the key words *Pray, God's Name, God's Day, Obey, Respectful, Kind, Truthful,* and *Honest* for the commandments. After the other family members have found them, arrange them in order.

6. Get ten 3 x 5 cards or slips of paper and print on them "God comes first!" You and your children can decorate these and put them in prominent places around the house for the day. When your celebration day is over, leave one of these cards up in a place where you can all see it every day.

Family Feature

Guideposts to God

Your child has learned that following the commandments leads to our freedom and our happiness. To help underscore the lesson of how the commandments help free us from the trouble that sin causes, discuss the following situations and ask the questions that follow.

1 Think of a situation where a TV or movie character disobeys his or her parents and gets into trouble.
(Fourth Commandment)

2 Discuss a movie or TV show where somebody takes what doesn't belong to him or her.
(Seventh Commandment)

3 Think of a movie or TV show where one of the characters isn't kind to another person.
(Fifth Commandment)

4 Talk about a movie or TV show where a character wants something someone else has and this makes him or her unhappy.
(Tenth Commandment)

Once you and your child have identified an example of a story you're familiar with ask, "Why is the person unhappy?" and "What needs to change so the person will be happy?" Make the connection to the commandment. The commandments are meant to afford us our own deep gladness in life. Follow this process for each of the four situations suggested.

You can make this kind of questioning a habit when you are watching television or movies or reading books together. It's a way to connect the moral lessons your child is learning to the gift of the commandments given to us by God, who longs for our freedom and our deep happiness.

Visit **www.ChristOurLife.org/family** for more family resources.

Jesus Gives Us the Gift of Peace

Peace I leave with you; my peace I give to you.

John 14:27

A Letter Home

Dear Parents and Family,

The Gospel provides great evidence of God's immense love for sinners. This is something to celebrate, considering we all stumble and fall from time to time. Jesus continues to extend his forgiving love to us in the Sacrament of Reconciliation.

Each chapter in Unit 3 prepares the children for their first Reconciliation by leading them to a deeper relationship with the Lord, as well as to reconciliation with him when they have failed to love.

In the unit, the children will reflect on how Jesus forgave Zacchaeus when the wealthy tax collector expressed his sorrow for cheating people. They will discover God's joyful acceptance of our own prayers for forgiveness. Consider the climate for forgiveness in your family. What do you do in your home to encourage a spirit of forgiveness?

The unit presents sin as saying "no" to God, who asks us to love and serve him and to be kind to others. We can experience God's forgiving love when we confess our sins in sorrow and demonstrate our desire to live faithfully and follow the teachings of the Church.

The unit concludes by teaching the children the steps of a good confession: examining their conscience, confessing their sins, praying an act of contrition, and doing the penance the priest asks of them. The children will then be ready to celebrate this sacrament that restores us to wholeness.

At the end of five of the chapters in this unit, the children will bring home a review of the chapter along with the "Building Family Faith" feature. At the end of the unit, the children will bring home a Family Feature handout to help nurture the family's faith at home.

Visit **www.ChristOurLife.org/family** for more family resources.

Our Friend Jesus Forgives Us

Jesus Chose Us to Be His Friends

We choose our friends. Friends are happy together. They share with one another.

Jesus chose us to be his friends. He wants to share his life and love with us. Jesus wants to share his heavenly home too. He said,

"You are my friends if you do what I command you."

(John 15:14)

Jesus tells us to love God our Father. He tells us to love others.

Jesus Is Always Our Friend

Jesus always loves us, but we do not always love our friends.

Sometimes we are selfish.

Then we are not good friends.

We say we are sorry.

Then we become friends again.

Jesus is always our friend. Sometimes we do not act like good friends of Jesus. We choose to do things he does not like. We fail to love God our Father. We fail to love others.

We tell Jesus we are sorry.

Jesus Forgave Zacchaeus

Number the pictures in the right order. Tell the story of Zacchaeus from Luke 19:1–10.

Jesus forgave Zacchaeus when he was sorry. Jesus forgives us when we are sorry. He shares his peace and joy with us. We try to be better friends of Jesus by being more loving toward others and trying to help them.

Jesus Forgives Us

Zacchaeus often cheated people. He changed when he met Jesus.

He made a good choice. He chose to follow Jesus. He became a friend of Jesus.

We make choices too. We can choose to be a friend of Jesus. We can be loving and kind to others. We can obey the commandments. These are good choices.

Sometimes we make bad choices. We hurt our friendship with Jesus. When we tell Jesus we are sorry, he forgives us. Then we are his friends again.

A Moment with Jesus

Think about a choice that you made today. Was it a good choice or a bad choice? Talk about it with Jesus.

Ask Jesus to help you make good choices all the time, even when it is hard.

Tell Jesus how much you love him. Thank him for being your friend.

We Can Choose to Be Friends of Jesus

Draw a smiley face next to the good choices and a sad face next to the bad choices.

○ Nikki helped her little sister with her homework.

○ Elizabeth stole candy from a store.

○ Mia played quietly while the baby was sleeping.

○ Jason took his sister's doll without asking.

○ Miguel visited his uncle in the hospital.

○ Frances broke a window and ran away.

○ Linda talked back to her mother.

○ Lupe helped deliver food to the food pantry.

Second graders wrote these notes.

Dear Greg,
I am sorry for the bad words that I called you. I really never meant them.
Love,
Jimmy

Dear Samantha,
I'm sorry I hurt your feelings. Please forgive me. This summer I will invite you to my party.
Love,
Marta

We Remember

When are we friends of Jesus?
Jesus said,

"You are my friends if you do what I command you."

(John 15:14)

We Respond

Jesus, I want to be your good friend. Be with me to help me love God my Father and other people.

Write a good choice you will make today.

_____

– – – – – – – – – – – – – – – – –

_____

Building Family Faith

NO MATTER WHAT we do, Jesus is always ready to be our friend. Through Jesus we see that God calls sinners to receive his forgiveness and peace. Jesus invites us to a change of heart.

REFLECT
"When Jesus came to the spot, he looked up and said, 'Zacchaeus, hurry down. I mean to stay at your house today.'" (adapted from Luke 19:5)

DISCUSS AS A FAMILY
• Zacchaeus welcomed Jesus into his home. How do you welcome Jesus into your home?
• What are the ways you ask for and offer forgiveness in your family?

PRAY
O my God, help me welcome you into my heart.

DO
• Take a nature walk or visit a natural history museum. Share how things you see speak of God's greatness.
• After a meal discuss God's gifts to you that day. Take turns praying grace and thanking God for particular gifts.
• Review with your child pages 2 and 3 in the Reconciliation Booklet.
• Pray with your child the Act of Contrition on the inside back cover of the student book and help him or her commit it to memory.

Visit **www.ChristOurLife.org/family** for more family resources.

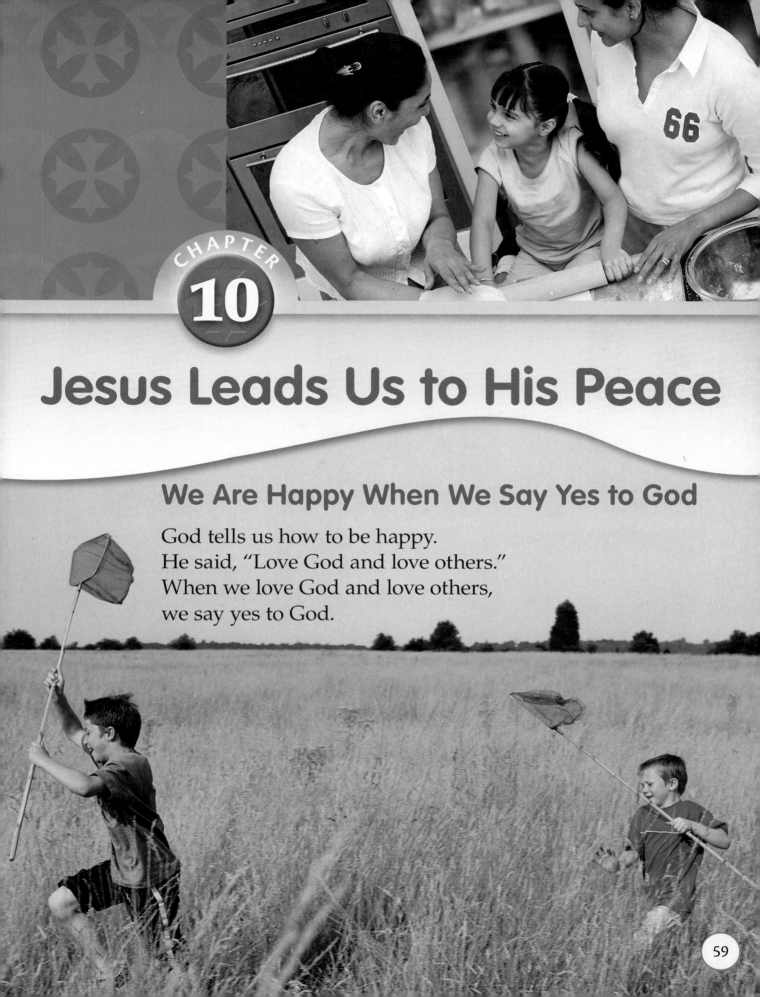

Jesus Leads Us to His Peace

We Are Happy When We Say Yes to God

God tells us how to be happy.
He said, "Love God and love others."
When we love God and love others,
we say yes to God.

We Need Jesus' Forgiveness

When we choose to be selfish and fail to love God and others, we say no to God. We commit a **sin**. We need forgiveness from God and his family.

Sometimes we think about doing something that is wrong. This is called **temptation.** Temptation is not a sin. We sin on purpose when we choose to do what is wrong.

Print a Y in the circle if the picture shows children saying yes to God.

Circle what sin is:

a temptation   saying no to God

an unloving act   a mistake   an accident

Jesus Gives Us the Sacrament of Penance and Reconciliation

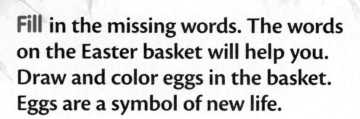

Fill in the missing words. The words on the Easter basket will help you. Draw and color eggs in the basket. Eggs are a symbol of new life.

On the evening of the first _____
Sunday, Jesus went to see the apostles.

He said to them, " _____ be with you."

The apostles were filled with joy to see _____ _____ .

Jesus said: "Receive the Holy Spirit.
Whose sins you forgive are forgiven them."

adapted from John 20:19–23

gift
Jesus
Easter
peace

Jesus gives us the **Sacrament of Penance and Reconciliation**.
In this sacrament we become friends of Jesus again. Our sins are forgiven.
We call this **reconciliation**. Reconciliation means to make up with
someone we have hurt. We ask for Jesus' forgiveness and he gives it to us.

Reconciliation was Jesus' Easter _____ to us.

Jesus Leads Us to His Peace CHAPTER 10 (61)

Jesus Forgave the Woman Who Had Sinned

A woman who had sinned came to Jesus while he was eating. She was sorry for her sins and began to cry. Jesus looked at her with love.

Simon and the other people at the table were not pleased. They thought Jesus should not let a sinner touch him. Jesus said to them, "She has loved more than you. Her sins have been forgiven."

Then Jesus told the woman, "Your sins are forgiven. Go in peace."

adapted from Luke 7:36–50

The woman would try to be a good friend of Jesus. She knew Jesus would help her.

A Moment with Jesus

Sit quietly knowing Jesus is with you. Jesus sent the Holy Spirit to the apostles. He sends the Holy Spirit to us too.

The Holy Spirit helps us when we're tempted to do wrong. The Spirit helps us ask for forgiveness and forgive others. Thank Jesus for this gift of the Holy Spirit.

Mistakes and Sins

The world is not right when people sin. Sin destroys peace.
How many things can you find wrong in this picture?

KEEP OFF GRASS

Circle Yes or No.

1. Do we love God when we fail to keep his laws? **Yes** or **No**

2. Do we love God when we tell him we are sorry? **Yes** or **No**

3. Does Jesus forgive us when we are sorry? **Yes** or **No**

4. Do we have peace after Jesus forgives us? **Yes** or **No**

5. Did Jesus give his apostles the power to forgive sins? **Yes** or **No**

6. Is temptation a sin? **Yes** or **No**

7. Did Jesus give us the Sacrament of Baptism on Easter Sunday? **Yes** or **No**

We Remember

What is sin?
Sin is choosing to say no to God and doing what is wrong on purpose. Sin offends God and hurts others and ourselves.

When does Jesus forgive our sins?
Jesus forgives our sins when we are sorry.

Words to Know

reconciliation
Sacrament of Penance and Reconciliation
sin   temptation

We Respond

God, I am sorry for all my sins. With your help I will try not to sin again. Amen.

Building Family Faith

JESUS CONTINUALLY CALLS us who have sinned to reconciliation. In the Sacrament of Reconciliation he gives us a sign of his divine forgiveness and leads us to greater peace.

REFLECT
Jesus came and stood in their midst and said to them, "Peace be with you."
(adapted from John 20:19)

DISCUSS AS A FAMILY
• How does saying we are sorry when we are wrong help heal a broken relationship?
• Discuss how in the Sacrament of Reconciliation the priest forgives us in Jesus' name, brings us God's peace, and helps us know what we can do to be more loving.

PRAY
Lord, have mercy. Christ, have mercy.
Lord, have mercy.

DO
• Help your child print his or her own "I'm Sorry" prayer on page 9 of the Reconciliation Booklet.
• Talk about times you needed to be forgiven. When you asked for and received forgiveness, how did it help you be more loving?
• Show your child the reconciliation room or confessional in your church.

The Holy Spirit Helps Us

The Holy Spirit Is with Us

Jesus said,

"I will send my Spirit to be with you always."

adapted from John 14:16

"The Holy Spirit will teach you."

adapted from John 14:26

We received the Holy Spirit when we were baptized. The Spirit helps us love God and one another.

We are kind and fair to everyone. We pray for other people. We also help and obey our parents.

God the Holy Spirit is within us. He helps us share his love, peace, and joy with others.

The Holy Spirit Helps Us Look into Our Hearts

The Holy Spirit helps us look into our own hearts. We ask him to help us know how we have loved God and others. The Holy Spirit also helps us know how to love God and others better.

We thank Jesus for the loving things he helped us do. We tell Jesus we are sorry for the unloving things we did. Then Jesus forgives us. He gives us his love, peace, and joy. We are happy.

Write a prayer to the Holy Spirit. Ask him to help you look into your heart.

_____

- -

_____

- -

_____

- -

_____

- -

_____

- -

When we look into our hearts, we can ask ourselves two big questions.

Write your answer to the first question on the line below.

How have I loved God?

_____

- -

_____

Draw your answer to the second question in the space below.

How have I loved others?

A Moment with Jesus

Imagine yourself in a quiet place.

Then think about all you have done today. How have you shown love for God? In what ways did you show love for your family and friends?

Jesus knows you want to be good. He knows how hard you try. Jesus loves you.

Review

Each Day We Can Look into Our Hearts

Find the unloving words in the heart. Put an X through them.

truthful respect

fight love lies

care help obey

honest selfish

mean words

share

We Remember

What does the Holy Spirit do for us?

The Holy Spirit helps us love God and one another. He helps us look into our hearts.

We Respond

Come, Holy Spirit, fill my heart with your love.

Building Family Faith

THE HOLY SPIRIT is with us always and helps us see when we are loving and when we are not. Because of the Holy Spirit, our lives can be filled with love, peace, and joy.

REFLECT
"The Advocate, the holy Spirit that the Father will send in my name—he will teach you everything and remind you of all that [I] told you."
(John 14:26)

DISCUSS AS A FAMILY
• Discuss the importance of taking time each day to listen to the Holy Spirit.
• How do we know that the Holy Spirit is inviting us to do something good?
• What are some signs that show we are following the Holy Spirit's guidance?

PRAY
Come, Holy Spirit, fill our hearts with your love.

DO
• Tell your child about a time you changed because you experienced the inspiration of the Holy Spirit.
• Help your child form the habit of looking into his or her heart each day to recognize acts of love or failures to show love.
• When your child quarrels with a friend, gently reflect together on the reasons for the quarrel and discuss ways to handle future situations.

Visit **www.ChristOurLife.org/family** for more family resources.

We Meet Jesus in the Sacrament of Reconciliation

We Like Being with People We Love

We enjoy seeing people we love. We like doing things with them and sharing our stories. When we are with them, we are happy.

Here are some of the things I like to do with my family and friends.

I like going on the back hill with my friends.

Jesus Forgives Us

Jesus liked being with children when he lived on earth. He loved them and blessed them.

Today we can meet Jesus in the Sacrament of Reconciliation. We meet him through the priest, who acts in Jesus' place. Jesus blesses and forgives us through the priest. We are forgiven.

We Confess Our Sins

"Child, your sins are forgiven."

(Mark 2:5)

"I am the light of the world. Whoever follows me will have life."

(adapted from John 8:12)

First, we admit we did something wrong. We tell our sins to the priest. We call this **confession.** No matter what we tell the priest, he keeps it a secret.

The priest then tells us how we can make up for our unloving act. Sometimes we say a prayer. Sometimes we do a good deed. This is our **penance.** It helps us stay away from sin. It also helps us become better people.

Before we confess, we pray to the Holy Spirit for guidance. The Spirit helps us make a good confession and live holy lives.

We Know These Words

Draw lines to match the words with their definitions.

1. priest ⬤   ⬤ a wrong act I choose to do

2. penance ⬤   ⬤ forgiveness

3. pardon ⬤   ⬤ person who acts in Jesus' place

4. sin ⬤   ⬤ telling my sins to the priest

5. confession ⬤   ⬤ a way of making up for my sins

We Can Do This

In the box below, write as many loving actions as you can.

A Moment with Jesus

Think of how much Jesus loves you. No matter what you do, he loves you. He always forgives you when you are sorry for doing wrong. Thank Jesus for his great love and for his forgiveness.

Print each word from the rainbow where it belongs in a sentence.

‾‾‾‾‾‾‾‾‾‾‾‾‾

– – – – – – – – – – –

1. I ‾‾‾‾‾‾‾‾‾‾‾

   to the Holy Spirit.

2. I confess my sins to the

   ‾‾‾‾‾‾‾‾‾‾‾‾‾‾‾

   – – – – – – – – – – – – –

   ‾‾‾‾‾‾‾‾‾‾‾ .

3. The priest gives a

   ‾‾‾‾‾‾‾‾‾‾‾‾‾‾‾

   ‾‾‾‾‾‾‾‾‾‾‾‾‾ .

   – – – – – – – – –

4. The priest ‾‾‾‾‾‾‾‾‾

   me in Jesus' name.

   ‾‾‾‾‾‾‾‾‾

   – – – – – – –

5. I go in ‾‾‾‾‾‾‾‾‾ .

penance

peace

priest

pray

forgives

We Remember

Who forgives our sins?

Jesus forgives our sins in the Sacrament of Reconciliation.

Words to Know

confession

penance

We Respond

Jesus, I'm sorry for my sins.

Building Family Faith

THROUGH THE SACRAMENT of Reconciliation, God forgives us whenever we confess our sins and express our desire to be more faithful to the teachings and examples of Jesus.

REFLECT

"Go first and be reconciled with your brother, and then come and offer your gift." (Matthew 5:24)

DISCUSS AS A FAMILY

• When we accept signs of love from those who ask forgiveness, we change sad and heavy hearts to ones of joy.

• Our smiles and our concern for others are often the most precious gifts we can give others.

• It is important to be willing and able to say "I'm sorry" to others and really mean it.

PRAY

Jesus, I am sorry for the times I fail to follow your ways.

DO

• Gently ask your child how he or she hurts others and offends God.

• Encourage your child to apologize when it's called for. Set an example by saying you're sorry when you do something wrong.

• Discuss page 15 in the Reconciliation Booklet. Explain how to express sorrow and do penance.

Visit **www.ChristOurLife.org/family** for more family resources.

CHAPTER 13

We Become Better Persons

God Forgives and Helps Us Be Better

Once King David did something that displeased God. He told God he was sorry. David said:

Forgive me, O God, in your goodness.

I have sinned against you. I have done what is wrong.

Take away all my sins. Put a new heart in me.

Fill me with joy and gladness. Make me willing to obey you.

adapted from Psalm 51:1–14

God forgave David and helped him be a better person. David praised and thanked God.

73

We Are Sorry for Our Sins

In the Sacrament of Reconciliation, the priest helps us do what David did. He tells us how to make up for being unloving. He tells us how to be more like Jesus.

We listen to the priest. We tell God we are sorry. We pray the Act of Contrition. **Contrition** is being sorry for what we have done wrong. The priest then says the words of **absolution.** These are the words of forgiveness. We praise and thank God for his goodness. We try to be better people.

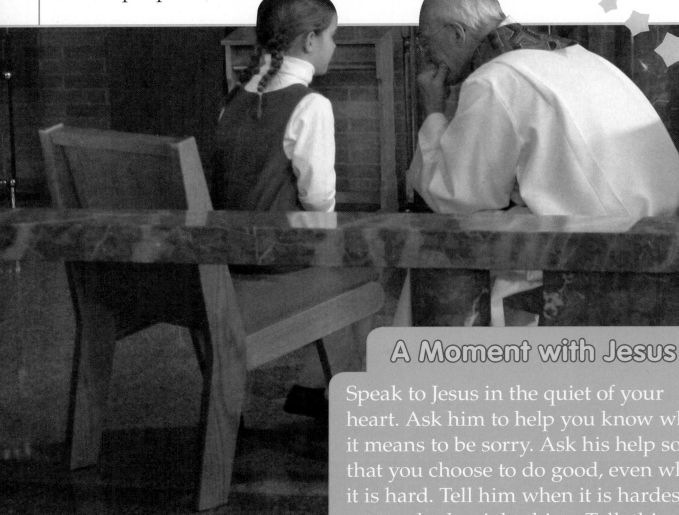

A Moment with Jesus

Speak to Jesus in the quiet of your heart. Ask him to help you know what it means to be sorry. Ask his help so that you choose to do good, even when it is hard. Tell him when it is hardest for you to do the right thing. Talk this over with Jesus. He always understands. He always forgives.

Steps to Remember When Celebrating the Sacrament of Reconciliation

1. The priest greets you, and you make the Sign of the Cross.
2. The priest may read aloud from the Bible.
3. You confess any sins.
4. The priest gives you a penance. It may be a prayer or a good deed to do.
5. You pray the Act of Contrition.
6. You make the Sign of the Cross silently when the priest gives you absolution, and you answer "Amen."
7. When the priest says "Go in peace," you thank him and leave.

You do the penance the priest has given you.

Write **in each circle the number of the step that goes with the word.**

- ⬤ confession
- ⬤ tell God you are sorry
- ⬤ helps make up for sins
- ⬤ forgives

Park the cars in their correct garages. Match the words with their definitions.

 contrition

 Saying "I forgive you"

 penance

 Saying "I'm sorry"

 absolution

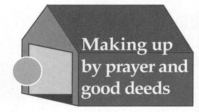 Making up by prayer and good deeds

Words to Know

contrition   absolution

We Remember

What does Jesus do for us in the Sacrament of Reconciliation?
Jesus forgives us, gives us peace, and helps us become better people.

What is the most important thing for us to do in the Sacrament of Reconciliation?
The most important thing is to be sorry for our sins.

How do we make up for our sins?
We do a penance. It may be prayers or good deeds.

We Respond

Give thanks to the LORD, who is good, whose love endures forever.

Psalm 118:1

Building Family Faith

OUR GOOD GOD forgives us over and over. Each time we experience the wonder of his mercy we are moved to response with thanks and praise.

REFLECT
Create in me a clean heart, O God, and put a new and right spirit within me.
(adapted from Psalm 51:12)

DISCUSS AS A FAMILY
- What are some ways that a person can make up for a sin?
- God longs to forgive us no matter what it is that we do.
- Discuss the importance of telling God that we are sorry when we sin.

PRAY
Lord, your mercy endures forever.

DO
- Practice forgiving your child with a generous heart in order to model God's bountiful mercy.
- Help your child memorize the Act of Contrition. It can be found on the inside back cover of this book.
- Review the Reconciliation Booklet with your child. Make sure he or she can discuss the sacrament with confidence.

Visit **www.ChristOurLife.org/family** for more family resources.

Jesus Calls Us His Friends

We Are Friends of Jesus

Mary and Martha were friends of Jesus. Mary listened to Jesus tell about his Father's love. Martha was kind to Jesus. She sometimes cooked for him.

We are friends of Jesus too. He wants us to listen to him as Mary did. He wants us to learn about his Father's love. He wants us to be kind like Martha. He wants us to share his Father's love.

Jesus Cares for His Friends

Match the words with the pictures. Put the number in the circle. Tell the story that goes with the picture.

1. The Lost Sheep
2. A Sinful Woman
3. Apostles
4. Jesus
5. The Sacrament of Reconciliation
6. Zacchaeus

How Well Do You Remember?

Draw lines to complete each sentence.

The Holy Spirit helps us ◯   ◯ the priest gives us.

We are sorry and want
to make up for ◯   ◯ look into our hearts.

We do the penance that ◯   ◯ our sins.

The penance may be ◯   ◯ forgiveness and peace.

We praise and thank
Jesus for his ◯   ◯ prayers or good deeds.

Circle Yes or No.

1. Does Jesus love us even when we sin?   **Yes or No**

2. Does the priest forgive us in Jesus' name?   **Yes or No**

3. Can we receive Jesus' forgiveness when we are not sorry?   **Yes or No**

4. Do we sin when we are tempted to do wrong?   **Yes or No**

5. Does the priest act in Jesus' place when we celebrate
   the Sacrament of Reconciliation?   **Yes or No**

6. Are accidents sins?   **Yes or No**

7. Does Jesus forgive our sins in the Sacrament
   of Reconciliation?   **Yes or No**

8. Do our sins hurt God's family?   **Yes or No**

9. Do we show love for God when we fail to keep his laws?   **Yes or No**

10. Does Jesus help us to love God and others
    through the Sacrament of Reconciliation?   **Yes or No**

Act of Contrition

Fill in the missing words.

My God,
I am _____ for my sins with
all my heart.
In _____ to do wrong
and failing to do _____,
I have _____ against you
whom I should love above
all things.

I firmly intend, with your help,
to do _____,
to sin no more,
and to avoid whatever leads me
to _____.
Our Savior, Jesus _____,
suffered and _____ for us.
In his name, my God, have mercy.

We Remember

In what sacrament does God
forgive our sins?

God forgives our sins in the
Sacrament of Reconciliation.

We Respond

Jesus, send the Holy Spirit to
guide me in doing good and
avoiding sin.

Peace and Forgiveness

Song

Leader: In the name of the Father, and of the Son, and of the Holy Spirit

All: Amen.

Leader: Praised be God, who forgives us when we are sorry.

Blessed be God forever.

All: Blessed be God forever.

Leader: Let us pray this song of King David, letting God know we are sorry for our sins.

All: Forgive me, O God, in your goodness.

Side A: I have sinned against you. I have done what is wrong.

All: Forgive me, O God, in your goodness.

Side B: Take away all my sins. Put a new heart in me.

All: Forgive me, O God, in your goodness.

Side A: Keep your holy Spirit within me.

All: Forgive me, O God, in your goodness.

Side B: Fill me with joy and gladness.

All: Forgive me, O God, in your goodness.

(adapted from Psalm 51:1–14)

We Celebrate

Leader: When we celebrate the Sacrament of Reconciliation, God forgives us. We meet Jesus and receive his peace. Let us share that peace with a friend.

All: *(Exchange a sign of peace.)*

Leader: Let us end our prayer as we began it, by praying the Sign of the Cross.

All: In the name . . .

Song

Family Feature

Peace in Our Homes

The Phans go as a family to celebrate the Sacrament of Reconciliation at their church. On the evening before, they meet together, and the family members ask forgiveness of one another for the times they failed to love. They read a story or passage from the Bible about sorrow for sin and God's loving mercy.

Family Feature

Mr. and Mrs. Phan bless their children. Then everyone prays the Our Father, holding hands. Sometimes they sing a song such as "Peace Is Flowing like a River."

On the day of the sacrament, the Phans hang a paper dove in the dining room as a reminder of the renewed peace they experience from forgiveness. After receiving the sacrament, the family celebrates by going to an ice-cream parlor or a pizza restaurant.

When your child receives the Sacrament of Reconciliation for the first time, you might wish to begin the tradition of a family reconciliation prayer service.

How to Make a Dove

1. Draw an outline of a dove on a sheet of paper and cut it out.

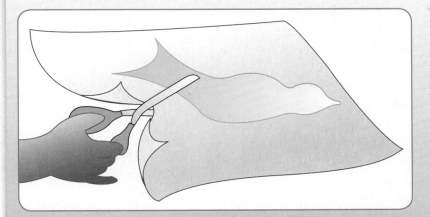

2. Make a slit in the dove's side. Accordion-pleat a sheet of thin paper.

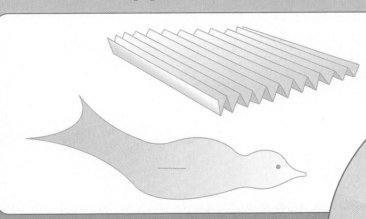

3. Insert the paper into the slit to make wings. To hang, tape the top part of the wings together and thread string through them.

A Family Reconciliation Celebration

(Have a crucifix available.)

Child: *(Lights a candle.)*

Parent: Jesus says:

> You are the light of the world. A city set on a mountain cannot be hidden. Nor do they light a lamp and then put it under a bushel basket; it is set on a lampstand, where it gives light to all in the house. Just so, your light must shine before others, that they may see your good deeds and glorify your heavenly Father.
>
> Matthew 5:14–16

Parent: One of the best things about being a family is that we always belong. Even when we hurt somebody else in the family, we still belong. But when we hurt somebody in our family, we feel unhappy, and our family is not together as it should be. So tonight we pray together and tell one another that we will try to be more loving and more forgiving.

All: *(Join hands and pray the Our Father.)*

All: *(Everyone takes a turn to tell something the others do that makes him or her happy.)*

Parent: In the Sacrament of Reconciliation, God our Father brings us closer together with all the members of our family. Jesus tells us how we can be reconciled to one another. This year [name of child] celebrates the Sacrament of Reconciliation for the first time. In the sacrament, we tell the priest how we have failed to love and how we want to change our hearts as Zacchaeus did. Let us pray that we will be more loving after we meet Jesus in the Sacrament of Reconciliation.

All: Stay with us, Lord, and be our joy!

Visit **www.ChristOurLife.org/family** for more family resources.

Jesus Gives Us the Gift of Himself

I am the living bread that came down from heaven; whoever eats this bread will live forever.

John 6:51

A Letter Home

Dear Parents and Family,

God is always reaching out to us to show us his love. Now, your child will discover another expression of this love: the Holy Eucharist.

Each chapter in Unit 4 will increase the children's awareness of Jesus' love and help them participate meaningfully in the celebration of the Eucharist. They will become familiar with the parts of the Mass so they can participate more fully in the liturgy. They will be prepared to receive their First Communion with love and joy.

The children will learn that during his Last Supper, Jesus gave the Church the means to join him in joyful praise of the Father. Through the Church, the Mass brings Christ's love and his sacrifice to us in sacramental form. The children will learn how to offer themselves with Jesus' sacrifice at Mass and how the Bread of Life unites them with God and with one another.

Next, the children will hear how the Body and Blood of Christ becomes present under the form of bread and wine at the consecration during the Mass. They will be taught to prepare to receive Jesus reverently. They also will be encouraged to show gratitude for God's gift by serving others and sharing God's love with them.

At the end of each chapter in this unit, the children will bring home a review of the chapter along with the "Building Family Faith" feature. This feature gives you a quick review of what your child learned and offers practical ways to reinforce the lesson at home so that the whole family may benefit. At the end of the unit, the children will bring home a Family Feature handout to help nurture the family's faith at home.

Visit **www.christourlife.org/family** for more family resources.

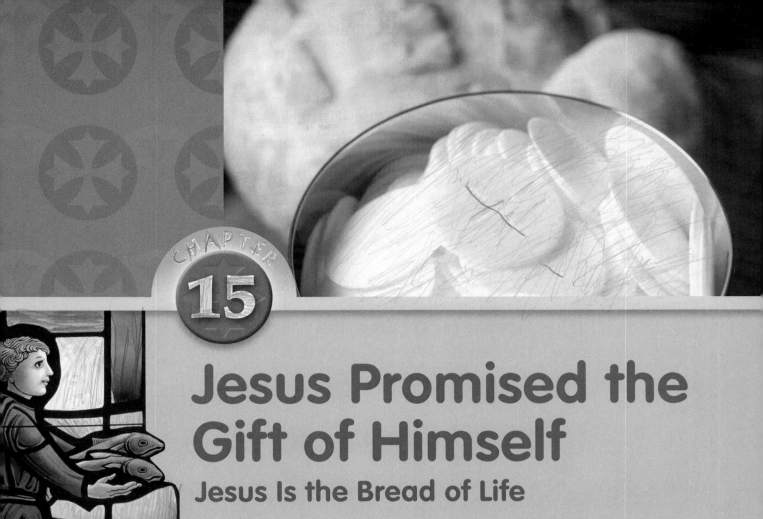

Jesus Promised the Gift of Himself

Jesus Is the Bread of Life

Jesus said,

"I am the bread of life; whoever comes to me will never hunger."

John 6:35

Jesus Fed the People

A big crowd of people followed Jesus. They stayed with him all day. Jesus knew they were hungry by the end of the day. He wanted to feed them.

A boy in the crowd had five loaves of bread and two fish. Jesus took them and gave thanks to God our Father. Then he shared the bread and fish with all the people. They all had as much as they wanted to eat. Twelve baskets of food were left over. Jesus had worked a **miracle.**

Jesus Promised to Give the Eucharist

The day after the miracle, the people found Jesus. He knew they had come because he had given them bread to eat.

He said to them, "You should work for bread that will help you live forever."

The people said, "Teacher, give us this bread always."

Then Jesus promised the gift of the Eucharist. He said,

"I am the living bread that came down from heaven; whoever eats this bread will live forever."

John 6:51

Many people did not believe Jesus. They asked, "How can he give us his body to eat?"

But the twelve apostles had faith. Peter said, "We believe."

Today Jesus Christ comes to us in the forms of bread and wine. We receive him in **Holy Communion.** We believe.

Write the words "I believe" on the line. Color and decorate the banner. You may draw jewels on the chalice and crosses on the hosts if you like.

Body and Blood of Christ

I be lieve

A Moment with Jesus

Jesus loves you. He invites you to share his life and love in a special way. He wants you to receive him in Holy Communion so that you can live with him forever in heaven. What do you want to say to Jesus?

Finish the sentences. Use the words on the bread.

The Eucharist is

Jesus Christ .

The sacred bread is his

Body .

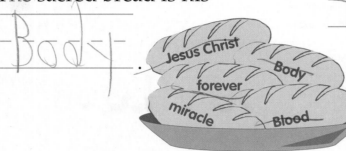

Jesus Christ
Body
forever
miracle
Blood

The sacred wine is his

Blood .

If we receive the Eucharist, we will live

forever .

We believe that Jesus can work this

miracle .

We Remember

What is the Eucharist?
The Eucharist is the sacrament in which we receive Jesus Christ.

We Respond

Lord, you have the words of eternal life. I believe.

Words to Know

Holy Communion   miracle

Building Family Faith

THE FOOD AND THE DRINK of the Eucharist is Jesus. He is the Living Bread, broken and shared to give God's life and love to the world.

REFLECT
"I myself am the living bread come down from heaven. If anyone eats this bread he shall live forever." (adapted from John 6:51)

DISCUSS
- It is important to eat together with family and friends. Recall favorite meals (elaborate or simple) that you have enjoyed together.
- How do the meals you eat as a family relate to the Eucharist shared at church?
- When we say "Amen" before receiving the Eucharist, it shows that we believe what Jesus says and that we want to obey God.

PRAY
Thank you, Jesus, for the gift of yourself.

DO
- Talk about why we come together for Sunday Mass—to worship and thank our Father with, through, and in Jesus.
- Find time to bake bread with your child. While the bread is baking and its aroma fills your kitchen, read John 6:51, pray the Our Father together, and discuss how bread gives life and nourishment. Then share the warm bread with your whole family.

Visit **www.ChristOurLife.org/family** for more family resources.

We Celebrate God's Love

God's People Celebrate Passover

Read each sentence and find the matching picture.

1. God's people were slaves.
2. The blood of a lamb saved God's people from death.
3. God's people celebrated a meal.
4. God freed his people.

Jewish people still celebrate **Passover** today.

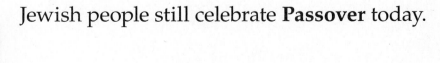

Jesus Celebrates a Special Meal

On the night before Jesus died, he celebrated Passover with his apostles. Before supper, Jesus got a basin of water and a towel. He began to wash the feet of each apostle. When he finished, Jesus said,

> "If I, your master and teacher, have washed your feet, you should do things like this for one another."

adapted from John 13:14–15

After that, he gave us a new commandment:

> "As I have loved you, so you also should love one another."

John 13:34

Jesus Gave the Gift of Himself at the Last Supper

At the **Last Supper,** Jesus took bread. He thanked and praised his Father. Then he blessed the bread and broke it. He gave it to the apostles and said,

> "Take this, all of you, and eat it. This is my body, which will be given up for you."

Then Jesus took the cup and blessed it. He shared the wine with them, saying,

> "Take this, all of you, and drink from it. This is the cup of my blood. It will be shed for you and for all so that sins may be forgiven."

Then Jesus said,

> "Do this in memory of me."

adapted from 1 Corinthians 11:23–25

At the Last Supper, Jesus offered the gift of himself to his Father. When he did this, he gave us the Mass.

At Mass, Jesus Gives Himself to the Father

Jesus has the greatest love for his Father and for us. Jesus gave himself to the Father as a **sacrifice** on the cross. A sacrifice is a gift given to God. Jesus gave up his life so that we could live with God forever.

The Mass is a gift that helps us remember and celebrate God's love.

At Mass, God speaks words of love to us. We listen to God's words. They tell us how we can give him gifts of love.

At Mass, Jesus offers himself to his Father for us. We offer the sacrifice of Jesus. We offer ourselves.

We can make everything we do a gift of love to God.

A Moment with Jesus

Thank Jesus for the great sacrifice he made for you on the cross. Think about a sacrifice you have made. Tell Jesus that you will offer your own sacrifice with his the next time you are at Mass. For now, offer your love to Jesus.

We Give Ourselves with Jesus

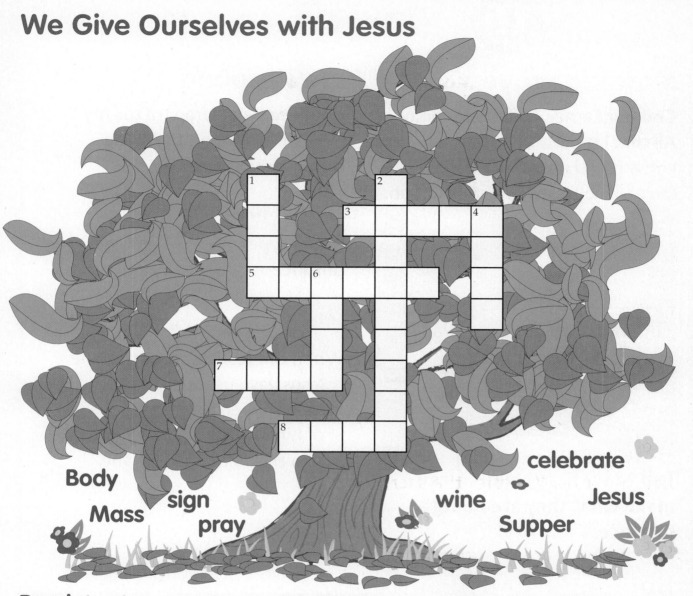

Body

Mass

sign

pray

celebrate

wine

Jesus

Supper

Read the clues. Use the words below the tree to fill in the puzzle.

Down

1. We offer the sacrifice of Jesus and ourselves to the Father at _____.
2. When we _____ the Mass, we offer the best sacrifice.
4. Every gift is a _____ of love.
6. We _____ with Jesus at Mass.

Across

3. _____ gave the best gift to God.
5. Jesus gave us the Eucharist at the Last _____.
7. At Mass, bread becomes Jesus' _____.
8. At Mass, the _____ becomes Jesus' Blood.

Morning Prayer

God our Father, I offer you today
All that I think and do and say.
I offer it with what was done
On earth by Jesus Christ, your Son.
Amen.

Tell how these children can make what they are doing a sacrifice.

We Respond

Jesus, help me prepare for my First Communion by loving others as you love me.

Words to Know

Last Supper   Passover
sacrifice

We Remember

When did Jesus give us the Mass?
Jesus gave us the Mass at the Last Supper. He offered the gift of himself to the Father and said, "Do this in memory of me."

Building Family Faith

THE MASS is a special meal at which Jesus offers himself to the Father. We join with Jesus in offering the gift of our lives to God.

REFLECT
"This is my body, which will be given for you; do this in memory of me."
(Luke 22:19)

DISCUSS AS A FAMILY
- At Mass, we don't just sit passively. With Jesus, we offer the moments of our lives to God.
- When you eat together as a family, you are fed physically, emotionally, socially, and spiritually. The same is true when you gather at the table of the altar.

PRAY
Give thanks to the Lord, for he is good!

DO
- At supper, share a thought, a word, or an act of the day that you offered to God.
- Ask your child to tell you about Passover. Talk about how God saved his people from slavery.
- When you help your child put on his or her socks or shoes, recall how Jesus washed the feet of his apostles as a sign of his love and service to them.

Visit **www.christourlife.org/family** for more family resources.

CHAPTER

17

Jesus Invites Us

We Come with Love and Joy

Jesus invites God's people to the Eucharist.

At the Last Supper, he said,

"Do this in memory of me."

Luke 22:19

Jesus wants people to celebrate his victory over sin and death. He wants people to praise and love the Father with him. Jesus wants children to come to his celebration too. He told his friends,

"Let the children come to me."

Luke 18:16

95

We Gather Together

The family of Jesus comes together to celebrate at Mass. We come to Mass to remember Jesus' dying and rising. We celebrate his great love and the love of our Father.

We greet others as we enter the church. Before taking our place, we genuflect to show our love for God.

The Mass begins when the priest and others walk to the **altar,** the table of the Lord. We praise God by singing together as his people.

Draw a picture of the altar in your church. Include the people and things you see around the altar.

We Ask for Mercy

Jesus makes us all one in God's family.
We come together to share the Eucharist.
This is the meal of love.

But sometimes we have not been
loving. We have brought unhappiness
to God's family.

We pray:

> I confess to almighty God and
> to you, my brothers and sisters,
> that I have sinned through my
> own fault.

Then we ask God to forgive us:

> Lord, have mercy.

> Christ, have mercy.

> Lord, have mercy.

The priest asks God to have mercy on us.
God forgives us, and we forgive one another.
We are ready to celebrate the Eucharist.

A Moment with Jesus

Remember that Jesus is always with you. Speak to him
in your heart. Share with him the times when you were
not as kind as you could have been. Let Jesus know
you are sorry. Then tell him the good things you do for
others. Jesus knows how hard you try, and he loves you
for it.

We Praise God

We praise God the Father, the Son, and the Holy Spirit.

On most Sundays and special days, we pray:

Glory to God in the highest and peace to his people on earth.

God is good to his people. We want to praise God in words and actions.

We Ask and God Hears

The priest prays and asks God to help us.

_____

_ _ _ _ _ _ _ _ _ _ _ _ _ _ _ _ _

We say _____ .

God hears our prayer.

God gives us many blessings.

We Celebrate at Our Church

Match the words with their meanings.

1. altar   2. Sunday   3. song   4. Mass

5. praise   6. genuflect   7. priest   8. Jesus' words

○ the Lord's Day

○ giving glory to God

○ "Do this in memory of me."

○ reverent touching of the knee to the ground

○ praying with music

○ table of the Lord

○ celebration of Jesus' sacrifice

○ leads us in celebrating Mass

Draw a picture of something that happens during Mass.
On the lines below, write what is happening in the picture.

We Remember

What do we celebrate at Mass?

At Mass, we celebrate Jesus' victory over sin and death.

Word to Know

altar

We Respond

We worship you.
We give you thanks.
We praise you for your glory.

The Mass

- Entrance Procession and Song
- Sign of the Cross
- Greeting
- Penitential Rite
- Glory to God
- Opening Prayer

Building Family Faith

WHEN WE GATHER at Mass, we enter into a sacred time. By praising God in song and prayer, and asking forgiveness, we prepare ourselves to be fully present before God.

REFLECT
The grace and peace of God our Father and the Lord Jesus Christ be with you. (*Jesus Gives Himself*, page 3)

DISCUSS AS A FAMILY
- It is necessary to prepare our minds and hearts before going to Mass by asking forgiveness of God and of others.
- Tell one another your favorite hymn to sing at church. Remind your child that singing is a form of praying.

Visit **www.ChristOurLife.org/family** for more family resources.

PRAY
Glory to God in the highest!

DO
- Pray the I Confess or Glory to God with your child each day until he or she can join the people at Mass.
- Help your child see that our actions carry messages about what is in our hearts. Tell how dressing appropriately for Mass, being on time, and looking at the priest and readers when they speak show our love for Jesus and our respect for others.
- Encourage others in the family by using words of praise.

CHAPTER 18

We Listen and Pray

We Listen to the Word of the Lord

When we listen to someone, we show respect for him or her. Listening shows that we love and care. We listen carefully when we want to hear.

God speaks to us at Mass in the two readings and in the Gospel. We want to hear what God says. God's words are important to us.

After the first reading, we pray a psalm. Then we listen to the second reading. After each reading, we say:

Thanks be to God.

We Listen to the Gospel

Now we get ready to hear the Gospel. We show our joy and sing Alleluia.

The priest or deacon says:

A reading from the holy Gospel according to

_____

– –

_____ .

We say: **Glory to you, Lord.**

The priest or deacon reads the Gospel at the **ambo.**
We listen to the Good News.
Then we say: **Praise to you, Lord Jesus Christ.**

The priest or deacon gives a homily. He speaks to us about the readings and the Gospel. He helps us love God and others more.

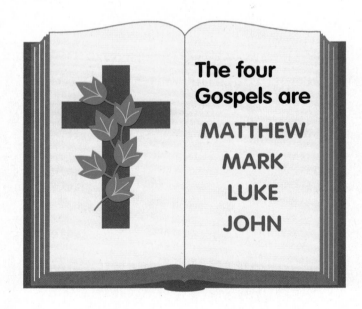

The four
Gospels are

MATTHEW

MARK

LUKE

JOHN

We Tell God We Believe

We believe in Jesus and in what he taught.

When we gather together at Sunday Mass, we pray the Creed. In the Creed, we say what we believe.

We believe in God the Father.
- ✤ He is almighty.
- ✤ He created heaven and earth.

We believe in Jesus Christ.
- ✤ He is God's only Son.
- ✤ He was born of the Virgin Mary.
- ✤ He died for us and was buried.
- ✤ On the third day, he rose again.
- ✤ He will come again.

We believe in the Holy Spirit.

We believe in the holy Catholic Church.

We believe that God forgives sins and that we will rise from the dead and live forever.

We Ask God for Help

These pictures show people with needs. Everyone has needs. What are some things we need?

Jesus cared about people. He helped people who were in need. Jesus' friends helped people in need.

When we love people, we show we care. We also help people in need. At Mass, we show we care. We pray for the Church and for our community. We pray for the needs of people everywhere and for ourselves. We pray:

Lord, hear our prayer.

Write on the lines your name and the name of someone you would like to pray for.

_____

- - - - - - - - - - - - - - -

_____

- - - - - - - - - - - - - - -

_____

A Moment with Jesus

Share with Jesus what you are learning about the Mass. Tell him whom you will be praying for the next time you are at Mass. Trust Jesus to care for the people you love. He will care for them and for you.

We Live God's Word

When we hear God's Word at Mass, we find out how we can live as his children.

Here are words from the Bible. Draw a line from each sentence to the picture it matches best.

"I was hungry and you gave me food."

adapted from Matthew 25:35

Children, obey your parents.

adapted from Ephesians 6:1

God loves a cheerful giver.

adapted from 2 Corinthians 9:7

Find the names of the four Gospels. Circle them. (Hint: One is diagonal.)

```
Z M M R P
L I A Q L
W O T R U
S T T M K
J O H N E
N V E C X
K U W P R
```

Number these parts of the Mass in order.

God Speaks

_____ Psalm

_____ First Reading

_____ Gospel and Homily

_____ Second Reading

_____ Alleluia

We Speak

_____ Prayer of the Faithful

_____ Creed

The Mass

✛ First Reading
✛ Psalm
✛ Second Reading
✛ Alleluia
✛ Gospel
✛ Homily
✛ Creed
✛ Prayer of the Faithful

We Remember

How does God speak to us at Mass?

God speaks to us at Mass through readings from the Bible.

Word to Know

ambo

We Respond

Lord, be in my mind, on my lips, and in my heart.

Building Family Faith

AT MASS, WE HEAR the Word of God proclaimed, and we respond with silent reflection and singing. The homily relates God's Word to our lives. We profess our faith.

REFLECT
Thanks be to God. (*Jesus Gives Himself*, page 6)

DISCUSS AS A FAMILY
- Explain that Scripture can speak in special ways to our hearts. At Mass, we listen with our minds and hearts to the readings and the Gospel.
- After Mass, discuss the ideas and themes you heard in the homily.

PRAY
Your Word, O Lord, is eternal.

DO
- Create bookmarks with your child to use in the family Bible. Decorate them with signs that show respect for God's Word.
- Have everyone in the family name a favorite Bible story. Act each story out and see who can guess which story it is.
- Look around your church and find symbols and characters from the Bible. Explain them to your child. If you are unsure, ask your pastor to explain.

Visit **www.ChristOurLife.org/family** for more family resources.

CHAPTER 19

We Prepare Our Gifts

We Bring Our Gifts

We bring gifts of bread and wine to the altar. We can bring other gifts too. Sometimes money is offered.

The gifts we have are signs of God's goodness to us. They are signs of ourselves. We offer these gifts to show God our love and to thank him for his goodness. We pray that God accepts our sacrifice.

We pray:
Blessed be God forever.

We Give Thanks and Praise

The priest invites us to thank God for his love. God has been very good to us. He made us. He gives us many gifts. Jesus is the best gift. It is right to give God thanks and praise. The word *Eucharist* means "giving thanks."

We Sing Holy, Holy, Holy

The priest invites us to join with the angels and saints in praising God. We sing or say:

Holy, holy, holy Lord, God of power and might. Heaven and earth are full of your glory.

At Mass, we celebrate with all God's people in heaven and on earth.

A Moment with Jesus

As you begin your prayer, imagine that all God's people on earth and all the angels and saints in heaven are praying with you. That's the way things really are. We are all one in God. Isn't it good to know that you have so many to help you follow Jesus! God is so good.

We Praise God in Our Words

Color the stained-glass window. Think about the story behind each symbol. Which one can you explain?

Draw a line to show what wheat becomes. Draw a second line to show what grapes become.

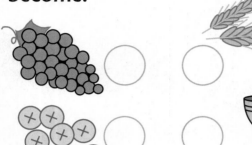

The Body of Christ

The Blood of Christ

Write the missing word:
Blessed be God

_____

— — — — — — — — — — — — .

The Mass

✠ **Preparation of the Altar and the Gifts**
✠ **Prayer over the Gifts**
✠ **Prayer of Thanks and Praise**
✠ **Holy, Holy, Holy**

We Remember

What are the bread and wine a sign of?

The bread and wine are a sign of God's goodness and a sign of ourselves. All that we have comes from and belongs to God.

We Respond

It is right to give God thanks and praise.

Building Family Faith

THE GIFTS of bread and wine we bring to the altar during Mass are signs that we want to offer to God the gifts of life and love he showers on us.

REFLECT
May the Lord accept the sacrifice at your hands for the praise and glory of his name.
(*Jesus Gives Himself*, page 10)

DISCUSS AS A FAMILY
• Talk about favorite gifts you've received that you are able to share with others. How does it feel to share gifts you've been given with others?
• Tell your child why you choose to support your local parish with your time, talent, and treasure. Talk about ways your child contributes to the life of the parish.

PRAY
Blessed be God forever!

DO
• Make a family banner to celebrate your child's First Communion.
• Volunteer to carry the gifts at Sunday Mass.
• Set aside time and make bread with your child.
• Read *A Birthday for Frances* by Russell and Lillian Hoban or *Mr. Rabbit and the Lovely Present* by Charlotte Zolotow and Maurice Sendak to lead into a discussion of gift giving.

Visit **www.ChristOurLife.org/family** for more family resources.

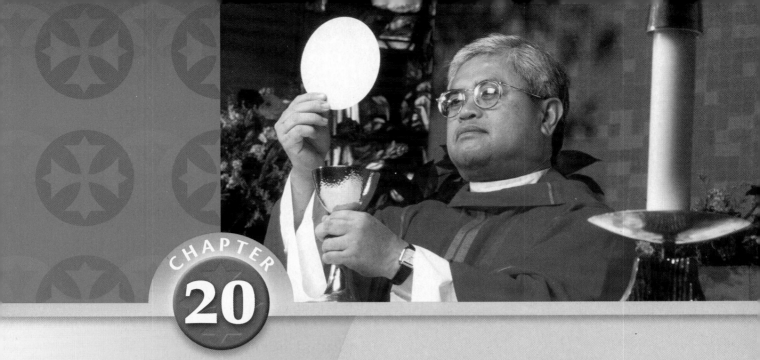

Jesus Offers Himself

THIS IS MY BODY

Jesus Gives Himself as a Sacrifice at Mass

The priest does what Jesus did at the Last Supper. He says:

> "This is my Body, which will be given up for you. This is the cup of my Blood. It will be shed for you."
>
> Eucharistic Prayer

Our gift of bread and wine becomes the **Body and Blood of Christ.** Jesus is with us in a special way.

Jesus Offers Himself with Love

Jesus is the perfect sacrifice. He offers himself to his Father with love. He offers himself for us.

Jesus told us to remember him. We remember:

Christ has died,

Christ is risen,

Christ will come again.

We Offer Ourselves with Jesus

With the priest, we offer Jesus to God our Father. We offer ourselves with Jesus.

We listen as the priest offers our gifts. Then he lifts up the host and the chalice. He praises the Father. We sing or say "Amen." Amen means we are saying yes to what the priest said.

A Moment with Jesus

Share with Jesus what you know about the word *Amen*. Did you mention that it means "yes"? Ask Jesus to help you make your whole life a big yes to God. Tell him how much you want to please God our Father. Then say "Amen."

We Remember What Jesus Christ Has Done

Fill in the blanks. Decorate the banner. Add fringe on the bottom.

We say:

_____

Christ has _____ ,

_____

Christ is _____ ,

_____

Christ will _____ again.

Jesus Gives Himself to the Father

Number the pictures in order.

 ◯ **Jesus on the cross**

 ◯ **Jesus at the Last Supper**

 ◯ **Jesus present in the Eucharist today**

The Mass
✣ **Eucharistic Prayer**
✣ **Consecration**
✣ **Doxology**
✣ **Great Amen**

We Remember

What is the perfect sacrifice?
Jesus is the perfect sacrifice, who offers himself at Mass.

Words to Know

Body and Blood of Christ

We Respond

My Lord and my God!

Building Family Faith

WE JOIN CHRIST in praising and thanking the Father in the Eucharistic Prayer of the Mass. We unite our daily sacrifices with Christ's perfect sacrifice to the Father.

REFLECT
Christ has died, Christ has risen, Christ will come again. (*Jesus Gives Himself*, page 14)

DISCUSS AS A FAMILY
- We appreciate giving gifts more when we put something of ourselves into the giving.
- We show special reverence during the consecration of the Mass because this is when Jesus Christ comes to us in a special way.

Visit **www.ChristOurLife.org/family** for more family resources.

PRAY
Heaven and earth are full of your glory.

DO
- At Mass, quietly remind your child when it is time for the Great Amen so that he or she can respond with the community.
- Help your child learn the Memorial Acclamations found on page 14 of the Mass Booklet *Jesus Gives Himself*.
- When you see your child acting kindly, being patient with others, or sharing, offer words of encouragement and praise.

CHAPTER 21

We Receive the Bread of Life

We Prepare to Receive Jesus

We pray the Lord's Prayer to ask forgiveness.
We show we are all brothers and sisters in God's family.

Jesus said:

"Peace I leave with you."

(John 14:27)

We give one another the sign of peace and say:

Peace be with you.

We ask Jesus to forgive us for the times we have upset the peace of God's family. We pray:

Lamb of God, you take away the sins of the world:
    have mercy on us.

The priest breaks the bread.

We think about the great love of Jesus. We think about how much more we could love. We look at the host and say:

Lord, I am not worthy to receive you.

Jesus Helps a Roman Soldier

Reader: The servant of a Roman soldier was sick in bed. The soldier loved his servant and took good care of him. The soldier went to Jesus to ask for help.

Soldier: Sir, my servant is very sick. He needs your help.

Jesus: I am sorry to hear that. I will come and heal him.

Soldier: *(kneeling)* Lord, I am not worthy to have you enter my home. Only say the word and my servant will be healed.

Jesus: *(lifting the soldier to his feet)* You have great faith. As you have believed, let it be done for you.

Soldier: Thank you. I know that it will be done.

Reader: At that moment the servant was healed. The soldier's family was happy and celebrated.

(adapted from Matthew 8:5–13)

This story helps us know how to prepare for Holy Communion.

Fill in the missing words. Use the words in the Word Bank.

When Jesus comes to us, he will

_____

— — — — — — — —

_____ us.

We will say, "Lord, I am

_____

— — — — — — —

not _____ to receive you, but only say

_____   _____

— — — — — — —   — — — — — — —

the _____ and I shall be _____."

Word Bank

worthy   help

healed   word

A Moment with Jesus

Think of the soldier's words to Jesus: "Lord, I am not worthy to have you enter my home." Tell Jesus this same thing in your own words. Jesus is pleased with your prayer. Listen in your heart to what he says to you. Then rest in his loving presence.

Jesus Comes to Us in Holy Communion

We have tried to love as Jesus does. We have fasted for an hour from everything except water and medicine. Now we are ready to receive Jesus.

We pray and sing while we wait. When it is our turn, the priest or extraordinary minister of Holy Communion shows us the host and says:

> The Body of Christ.

We bow and answer:

> Amen.

Then we may be offered the cup. The priest or extraordinary minister of Holy Communion says:

> The Blood of Christ.

We bow and answer:

> Amen.

We Thank Jesus for the Gift of Himself

The time after Holy Communion is special. We are united with Jesus and his family. Jesus is within us. Jesus, who loves us, has given himself to us.

We ask him to help us be **holy**, to live as God's children. We speak to Jesus in our hearts. We can tell him anything we wish.

We can say:

Jesus,

I **a**dore you.

I **l**ove you.

I **t**hank you.

I **a**sk you to . . .

I **r**esolve to . . .

What do the red letters spell?

_____

– – – – – – – – – – – –

_____

If you remember the letters that spell the word *altar,* you will know some things you could say to Jesus after Holy Communion.

Sometimes we pray silently after receiving Holy Communion. Sometimes we pray and sing our thanks to God together.

Receiving Holy Communion

Place your hands one on top of the other. The priest will put the host in your hand. Use your bottom hand to pick up the host and put it in your mouth. You can also put out your tongue far enough to receive the host.

The Mass

- ✠ The Lord's Prayer
- ✠ Sign of Peace
- ✠ Lamb of God
- ✠ Lord, I Am Not Worthy
- ✠ Communion
- ✠ Thanksgiving after Communion

We Remember

What do we do after receiving Jesus in Holy Communion?

We speak to Jesus in our hearts.

We thank him in prayer and song.

Word to Know

holy

We Respond

Lord, I am not worthy to receive you, but only say the word and I shall be healed.

Building Family Faith

THOSE PARTS OF the Mass that lead up to Holy Communion prepare us to receive the Body and Blood of Christ. This chapter describes the Mass prayers that prepare for Holy Communion and discusses personal prayer after Holy Communion.

REFLECT

"I am the living bread that came down from heaven; whoever eats this bread will live forever; and the bread that I will give is my flesh for the life of the world."

(John 6:51)

DISCUSS AS A FAMILY

- How does each family member pray during the time after Holy Communion?
- How can we thank Jesus for coming to us in the Eucharist?
- For what gifts are we grateful? What are we most grateful for today?

PRAY

Thank you, Jesus, for giving us yourself in Holy Communion. Come, Lord Jesus.

DO

- After dinner or at bedtime, read the story of the healing of the centurion's servant in Matthew 8:5–13.
- Practice with your child how to receive Holy Communion.

Visit **www.ChristOurLife.org/family** for more family resources.

CHAPTER
22

We Share God's Love with Others

We Love and Serve the Lord

Jesus loved and served God our Father. He shared God's love with others. He sent out his apostles to do this too.

The apostles went out and helped people. They taught people about God. They taught how to love God and one another.

At Mass the priest takes the place of Jesus. He blesses us and sends us out to do what Jesus and the apostles did. The priest says:

Go in peace to love and to serve the Lord.

We answer:

Thanks be to God.

We Celebrate the Eucharist

Match each picture with a sentence below. Write the correct letter under each picture.

A. We receive Jesus in Holy Communion and become one with God's family.

B. We listen to God speak to us.

C. The bread and wine become Jesus.

D. We bring gifts as signs of ourselves.

Some hosts from Mass are kept in the **tabernacle**. In this **Blessed Sacrament**, Jesus is always with us in our churches. He can be brought to sick people. We can visit him and tell him that we love him.

We Love and Serve the Lord in Many Places

We can love and serve God's people everywhere.

**Match the pictures and the words.
Put the correct letter in each circle.**

A. at home
B. at school
C. on the playground

D. on the street
E. in the world

Draw a smile ☺ if the answer is yes.
Draw a frown ☹ if the answer is no.

○ 1. Did Jesus give us the Mass at the Last Supper?

○ 2. Do we pretend that bread and wine are Jesus at Mass?

○ 3. Do Jewish people celebrate God's love at Passover?

○ 4. Does the Bible say that Jesus fed a crowd with a few loaves and fish?

○ 5. Did Jesus wash the apostles' feet to teach us how to love?

○ 6. Did Jesus offer himself to make up for his sins?

○ 7. Are we worthy to receive Holy Communion?

○ 8. Can we offer Jesus and ourselves to God the Father at Mass?

○ 9. Does God speak to us through the readings at Mass?

○ 10. Is a sacrifice a gift given to God?

The Mass

✛ Blessing
✛ Dismissal

We Remember

What may the priest say at the end of Mass?

The priest may say, "Go in peace to love and to serve the Lord."

We Respond

Thanks be to God.

Words to Know

tabernacle   Blessed Sacrament

The Lord Is Our Shepherd

Leader: Let us bless the Lord, now and forever.

All: Now and forever.

Leader: We have learned how Jesus gave us the gift of himself in the Sacrifice of the Mass. Let us listen once again to what he did.

Reader: A reading from the Gospel of Mark.

All: Glory to you, Lord.

Reader: While Jesus was eating with his friends, he took bread and said a blessing. Then he broke it and gave it to them, saying: "Take this. It is my body." Then he took a cup. He gave thanks and gave it to them. He said: "This is my blood, which will be shed for many people."

adapted from Mark 14:22–24

The Gospel of the Lord.

All: Praise to you, Lord Jesus Christ.

Leader: Let us give thanks for this great gift and pray:

The Lord is my shepherd, there is nothing more I need.

All: The Lord is my shepherd, there is nothing more I need.

Side A: You, Lord, are my shepherd. There is nothing more I need. You lead me to restful places and to streams of peaceful waters.

Side B: I may walk through dark valleys, but I won't be afraid, because you are with me.

Side A: You sit me at your table and give me food to eat. You fill my cup until it overflows.

Side B: Your kindness and love will be with me every day of my life. And I will live with you forever, Lord.

All: The Lord is my shepherd, there is nothing more I need.

Leader: Now let us go in peace.

All: Thanks be to God.

Song

Family Feature

Honoring the Eucharist

Long ago the Blessed Sacrament was sometimes carried in procession through the town to bless the people, into the fields to bless the land and the crops, and even into battles and disasters. Today the Ortiz family in Mexico looks forward each year to the feast of the Body and Blood of Christ, formerly called Corpus Christi. For this feast the family members join their neighborhood priests and friends in a grand outdoor procession. Maria Ortiz helps her mother set up an altar near their house. They cover it with fine linen. Her father practices the trumpet because he will be playing in the band that day.

Family Feature

On the feast day, priests in their finest vestments and people in their finest clothes walk behind the Eucharist which is contained in a gold and jeweled monstrance. The priest stops at the small altars along the way and blesses the people with the monstrance. Little Roberto Ortiz claps and cheers at the fireworks that add to the celebration.

In Spain, France, Italy, and Portugal on the feast of Corpus Christi, people use flower petals to make elaborate designs on the streets for the procession. In Austria, decorated boats carry the Eucharist across lakes, while worshipers follow in small boats.

Many Mexicans, as well as other immigrants to the United States, have brought their special customs honoring the Eucharist to their new parishes. In Holy Cross Parish in Chicago, the pastor carries the Eucharist as he leads a large procession of parishioners throughout the neighborhood, accompanied by music and singing. They stop at local playgrounds to pray, which has resulted in making these places safer for the neighborhood children.

In the United States the feast of the Body and Blood of Christ is celebrated on the Sunday after Trinity Sunday, which is usually in June. This year, when your child will receive First Communion, you can help foster a love and an appreciation for the Eucharist by celebrating it in your home. Here are a few suggestions:

- **Bake bread together and recall each family member's First Communion.** Bring out pictures, prayer books, and any other mementos of the day. Remind your child that Catholics all around the world receive the Eucharist, which is the Real Presence of Jesus Christ. People have been celebrating this special gift of Jesus' presence in the Eucharist for over two thousand years—ever since Jesus instituted this sacrament at the Last Supper.

- **Participate in Mass as a family and afterward have a festive breakfast.** To add to the enjoyment, have your child invite a friend to come along.

- **Check your parish schedule to see when exposition of the Blessed Sacrament is scheduled.** Spend time together in quiet prayer. This will be a great reminder for your child of the reverence we show toward Christ in the Eucharist.

Family Feature

Family Prayer Service to Bless the First Communicant

Setting: On the dinner table, set a candle, preferably your child's baptismal candle; a Bible opened to Luke 22:14–20; and a loaf of bread your child helped bake.

Parent/Leader:	This is a special night for _____ [child's name]. Tomorrow [he/she] will make [his/her] First Communion. Let us pray together as we light this candle.
Reader 1:	As you gave plentiful fruit and grain to Adam and Eve, our first parents, . . .
All:	You also give us food to eat, O Lord.
Reader 1:	As you cared for Noah and his family when the floods came and they sailed through the storm on the ark, . . .
All:	You also care for us, O Lord.
Reader 1:	As you provided manna and quail for the Israelites who wandered in the desert, . . .
All:	You also give us what we need, O Lord.
Reader 1:	As you fed the hungry crowds with the young boy's loaves and fishes, . . .
All:	You also accept our simple offerings, O Lord.
Reader 2:	*(Read Luke 22:14–20, the account of the Last Supper.)*
Parent/Leader:	We are like individual grains of wheat. Each of us is different, yet we are one family. As a sign of our unity and closeness as a family, let us share the bread that _____ [child's name] helped bake. *(Have the First Communicant give a piece of bread to each family member.)*
Parent/Leader:	_____ [child's name], this is the year when you receive Jesus in Holy Communion. But even now we welcome him in our hearts by sharing this bread as a family. We thank God for the gift of our daily bread and for the food with which he nourishes our bodies and souls. But most especially this evening we thank God for you, _____ [child's name]. May his grace be yours now and forever.
All:	Amen.

Visit **www.christourlife.org/family** for more family resources.

126d

The Church Celebrates God's Care

For in one Spirit we were all baptized into one body.

1 Corinthians 12:13

A Letter Home

Dear Parents and Family,

Our faith is an active and living thing. Unit 5 seeks to engage your child by introducing the ways the Church celebrates Christ's presence in the world.

The children will explore the roles of different members united in the Body of Christ, the Church. They will see how each member helps carry out God's plan and follows Jesus with the guidance of Church leaders. They will be encouraged to participate as members and to live as Christians, even during the summer, with the help of Christ's presence and Mary's prayers—as well as yours.

The children will find that the Eucharist unites all Christians within the Body of Christ, enabling them to make their lives an expression of Christ's love, no matter what vocation they live out. The Church has a mission, and each of us is challenged to share Christ's message, just as the apostles and early disciples did. The children will realize specific ways they can show Jesus' love to people. How might your family be challenged to do the same? There is never a shortage of opportunities to love.

Mary, Mother of the Church, has a unique role, interceding for her children and leading us closer to Jesus. The children will be shown how devotion to Mary can bring them closer to her Son.

At the end of two of the chapters in this unit, the children will bring home a review of the chapter along with the Building Family Faith feature. This feature gives you a quick review of what your child learned and offers practical ways to reinforce the lesson at home so that the whole family may benefit. At the end of the unit, the children will bring home the Family Feature to help nurture the family's faith.

Visit **www.ChristOurLife.org/family** for more family resources.

We Are One in the Church

The Church Is the Body of Christ

In one Spirit we were all baptized into one body.

adapted from 1 Corinthians 12:13

The Church is like a human body. It has a head and many parts. All the parts make up one body. It is the Body of Christ.

Each Christian is part of the Body of Christ. Each one helps the Church in a special way. In the Eucharist, Jesus helps us be one.

The Church Brings Us to Jesus

Jesus said,

"I am the good shepherd.
I have other sheep that do not belong
to this fold. These also I must lead.
There will be one flock, one shepherd."

adapted from John 10:14,16

Jesus has chosen good shepherds for
his Church.

✚ The pope is the Holy Father. He is the chief shepherd.
   He teaches all people about God's love.

_____

Our pope is named _____ .

✚ Bishops around the world help the Holy Father.

_____

Our bishop is named _____ .

✚ Priests help bishops.

_____

Our pastor is named _____ .

✛ **Deacons** are men called to serve the Church. They help the priests and bishops.

Deacons, brothers, sisters, and priests follow Jesus in a special way. Some serve in parishes. Some spend their days praying for the Church.

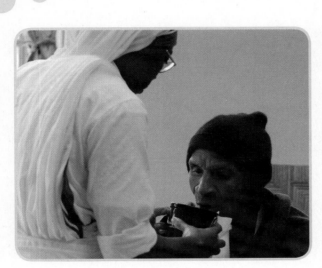

Some work as missionaries and spread the Good News near and far. All of them bring Jesus' love to many people.

A Moment with Jesus

Share with Jesus what you have just learned about how people serve the Church. Jesus might ask how you serve his Church. What do you answer? Jesus reminds you that every good act, no matter how little, and every prayer, whether short or long, helps God's people. Tell Jesus whatever is on your mind. Now just rest in his love.

The Church Teaches Us to Help

All members of the Church help others know Jesus' love.
You can help too.

Read the sentences. Find the missing words
in the purple box and print them on the lines.

This girl is making a

_____

— — — — — — — — —

_____

person happy.

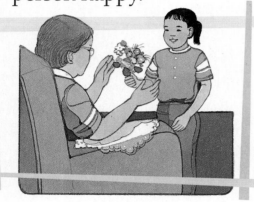

This boy is showing God's loving
care to a

_____

— — — — — — — —

_____ child.

These children are bringing
Jesus' joy to a

_____

— — — — — — —

_____ person.

This boy may be praying

_____

— — — — — —

for _____ people.

We Become like Jesus

We are one with Jesus. We try to become like him.

John Bosco helped others be one with Jesus. To do this, he started a club. Read the rules for his club and add two more to create a club of your own.

1. Never do anything that a child of God should not do.
2. Be cheerful about whatever you do.
3. _____

4. _____

Choose a name for your club and print it on the sign.

Put a + under the picture if you think the child in it is following club rules.

You are a member of the Body of Christ.
Color the balls that tell three things you will do in a special way this week.

We Remember

What is the Body of Christ?
The Church is the Body of Christ. Jesus is the head, and we are the members.

Word to Know

deacon

We Respond

Jesus, make me more like you.

Building Family Faith

THE CHURCH IS the Body of Christ, bringing Jesus' love to others and doing his work in the world. We all have a part in this work because we are all members of the Church.

REFLECT

Love is patient, love is kind. It is not jealous, [love] is not pompous, it is not inflated, it is not rude, it does not seek its own interests, it is not quick-tempered, it does not brood over injury, it does not rejoice over wrongdoings but rejoices with the truth.

(1 Corinthians 13:4–6)

DISCUSS AS A FAMILY

- A domestic family is one complete body too. How does the happiness of one person affect the whole family?
- How are we able to accomplish things together that we could not do alone?

PRAY

Bless your Church, Lord. Protect it. Make it strong.

DO

- Pray regularly for the needs of others. Make this a feature of dinnertime or bedtime prayers.
- Share something a family member said or did that brought you closer to God.
- Decide on a way your family can help someone in need.

Visit **www.ChristOurLife.org/family** for more family resources.

Mary, Mother of the Church, Cares for Us

Mary Asks Jesus to Help

Reader: Jesus and his apostles went to a wedding. Mary, the Mother of Jesus, was also there.

Everyone had a good time, but soon there was no more wine. Mary saw this and went to Jesus.

Mary: Son, they have no more wine.

Reader: Then she called the waiters.

Mary: Do whatever Jesus tells you.

Jesus: Fill the jars with water. Then give some to the chief waiter.

Reader: The waiter tasted it. It wasn't water anymore, but wine.

Waiter: You have saved the best wine until last!

adapted from John 2:1–11

Mary Is the Mother of the Church and Our Mother

Reader: Mary and the apostle Jesus loved stood near his cross. Then Jesus spoke to his mother.

Jesus: Here is your son.

Reader: Then Jesus spoke to his apostle.

Jesus: Here is your mother.

adapted from John 19:25–27

Mary is the Mother of Jesus' family, the Church. She watches over its leaders. She helps everyone in the Church know and love Jesus.

Mary is our Mother too. She watches over us with love. She takes care of us like she took care of the people at the wedding. She asks Jesus to give us what we need. Jesus listens to Mary.

A Moment with Jesus

Imagine you are standing with Mary at the foot of the cross. Jesus looks down at you and says, "Here is your mother." How wonderful! You have a heavenly mother to watch over, guide, and pray for you. Thank Jesus for this very special gift.

We Pray the Rosary

The Church honors Mary in prayer. A favorite prayer to Mary is the Rosary. Answer the questions below and then see how to pray the Rosary.

How many beads are in each group of small beads? _____
These groups are called decades.
How many decades are there? _____

Pray an Our Father on each large bead.

Pray a Hail Mary on each small bead.

Pray a Glory Be to the Father at the end of each decade.

Color the rosary. **Color the Hail Mary beads blue.**
Color the Our Father beads red.

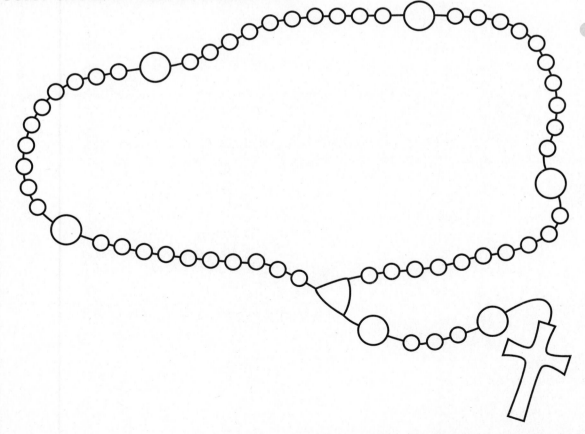

Use these words to tell a friend the story of Jesus' miracle at the wedding.

wedding	Mary	Jesus
wine	water	best

Then write an e-mail to Jesus, thanking him for the gift of his mother, Mary.

We Remember

Who is the Mother of the Church?

Mary is the Mother of the Church.

We Respond

Mary, Mother of the Church and our Mother, pray for us.

To: Jesus@email.com
Subject: A Thank-You Note to Jesus

Building Family Faith

JESUS' MOTHER, MARY, is our Mother as well. She cares for us, protects us, intercedes for our needs, and draws us closer to her Son, our Lord.

REFLECT

"Most blessed are you among women, and blessed is the fruit of your womb."

(Luke 1:42)

DISCUSS AS A FAMILY
- Mary helps us. What are the things that a mother does for her family?
- How can our Mother, Mary, help our family?

PRAY

Holy Mary, Mother of God, pray for us sinners.

DO
- Pray a decade of the Rosary as a family for the needs of your family.
- Locate a nearby shelter for women in crisis and involve your family in providing food or household items they may need.

Visit **www.christourlife.org/family** for more family resources.

CHAPTER 25

The Church Celebrates God's Love

Follow the path. **The letters tell how to get to heaven.**

Print them in the boxes below.

We can show our love for God in many ways.

We can think about him often.

We can choose to do what is right.

We can offer to help other people.

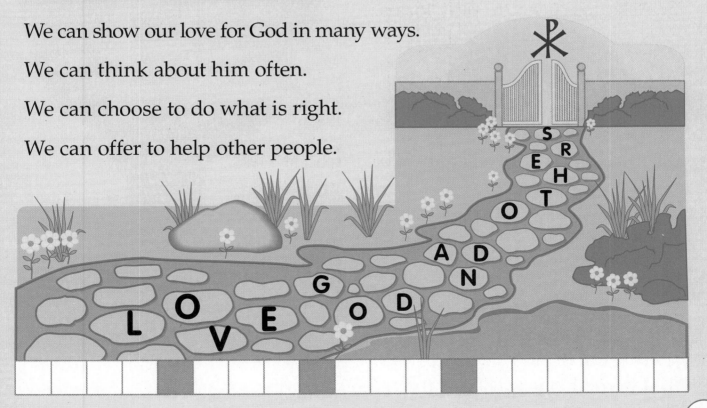

We Can Meet Jesus Today

Jesus loves us. He is always with us. He is most with us in the Church. He is present in his Word. We are close to him when we pray and go to Mass.

Pick a Word
The sentences here tell us things we can do to be with Jesus.

Print the words that are missing. **You can find them in the tree.**

1. _ _ _ _ each day.

2. Read the _ _ _ _ _ _ .

3. Ask _ _ _ _ to pray for us.

4. Be _ _ _ _ _ for sins.

5. _ _ _ _ _ _ when the Bible is read at Mass.

6. Receive Jesus in _ _ _ _ Communion.

7. _ _ _ _ our parents.

8. Ask the Holy Spirit to fill our hearts with _ _ _ _ .

This Is My Favorite Jesus Story

Page through your book to find a story Jesus told or a story about Jesus.

Draw a part of the story in each of the boxes. Share your picture story with your friends and family. Tell them what you learned from the story.

1

2

3

4

Use the words in the Word Bank to complete Jesus' promise.

Word Bank

heaven   eats

living   forever

No2

"I am the _____

bread that came down from

_____

_____.

_____

Whoever _____

this bread will live

_____

_____."

adapted from John 6:51

We Remember

What do Christians do?

Christians try to love God and others as Jesus did.

How do we know Jesus is with us?

Jesus said,

"I am with you always."

We Respond

Glory be to the Father, and to the Son, and to the Holy Spirit. As it was in the beginning, is now, and ever shall be, world without end. Amen.

God's Loving Care

Song

Child 1: When we were baptized, we became members of the Body of Christ, the Church. Because we belong to the Church, we met Jesus in the Sacrament of Reconciliation. We became one with him and others in Holy Communion. Today we thank Jesus for these signs of his love. We pray.

Leader: God our Father, look with love on your people. Pour out upon us your gifts so that we may lead others to you. We ask this through Christ our Lord.

All: Amen.

Reading

Reader: A reading from a letter of Saint Paul to the Ephesians. There is one Lord, one faith, one Baptism, and one God who is Father of all. Each of us has been given gifts to serve the Body of Christ. Jesus wants us to be one in what we believe about him. When each person does what God wants, the whole body grows. It becomes filled with love.

adapted from Ephesians 4:5,11–16

The Word of the Lord.

All: Thanks be to God.

Profession of Faith

Recite the Apostles' Creed on page 166.

Leader: Lord, we pray for these children who believe in you. May they enjoy the gift of your love, share it with others, and spread it everywhere.

Silent Reflection

Prayer

Leader: Let us turn to our Father in heaven, ask him to listen to our prayers, and say, "Father, hear our prayer."

Child 2: For the Holy Father, bishops, priests, deacons, religious sisters and brothers, and all who belong to the Church, that we may live joyfully as Christians.
[*Response*]

Child 3: For all the people of the world, that we may live as brothers and sisters who care about one another.
[*Response*]

Child 4: For our brothers and sisters who are hungry, sick, or in need, that our prayers and sacrifices may help them.
[*Response*]

Child 5: For those who do not yet believe in Jesus, that we may show them his love. [*Response*]

Child 6: For those who have sinned, that they may turn to God for forgiveness. [*Response*]

For all of us, that we may share God's love with one another. [*Response*]

Leader: Father, we have come before you with faith and love. Hear our prayers and let your Church serve you in peace and joy. We ask this through Christ our Lord. Amen.

Song

A Remembering Circle

At least once a year the Thomas family members gather for a remembering circle. This is an African-American custom that helps them understand their life history and see that all of our lives are woven together. We are all interdependent in living the Christian life.

Family Feature

The Thomas children, James and Kesia, arrange cushions or chairs in a circle in the family room. Mrs. Thomas makes a beautiful flower arrangement and sets it in the center of the circle along with a candle. Last fall she put branches of colorful leaves in a vase and made a circle of small vigil lights around it.

In the evening everyone in the family sits in the circle in the candlelight and thinks about people in their lives who have given them beautiful memories. These are people who have called forth their giftedness or those who have supported them by giving good advice, a shoulder to cry on, or a helping hand. They can be living or deceased, relatives, friends, or neighbors. Mrs. Thomas usually recalls something about her deceased grandmother, whom she affectionately calls "M'dear." This year James thought about Saint Anthony, who helped him find his dog, Spunky, when Spunky had run away.

Mr. Thomas remembered the doctor who set his broken leg and the friends who visited him in the hospital. Anyone who wishes may share a "remembering." After each remembering, the whole group prays, "We remember you in love for these good memories."

Saint Antonius
of Florence

144b

We Belong to the Communion of Saints

The Communion of Saints is one way to think about and to imagine the Church. This colorful phrase refers to both the holy elements (most especially the Eucharist) that God gives as a way to unite us, and the holy people we are united with. Pope Paul VI wrote, "We believe in the communion of all the faithful of Christ, those who are pilgrims on earth, the dead who are being purified, and the blessed in heaven, all together forming one Church; and we believe that in this communion, the merciful love of God and his saints is always [attentive] to our prayers." (Paul VI, *Creed of the People of God* 30. Cited in the *Catechism of the Catholic Church*, 962.)

You might begin the family tradition of a remembering circle in order to become more aware of what it means to belong to the Communion of Saints, the Church. It would be a good way to begin or end your family celebration of a holiday like Thanksgiving or New Year's Day.

Pope Paul VI

Family Feature

The Family Reunion

For most people, their most obvious connection with the Church is through their parish. But do you realize that as a family, you also participate in the domestic church, or church of the home? It is in the context of a loving home where faith is nurtured, forgiveness is learned, and the virtues are taught and practiced. The church of the home is where we are prepared to take our place at the table of the Lord in the larger community, and to live our faith in the world—on our jobs, in our neighborhoods, and as citizens.

Family-Gathering Activity

Get together as a family and take turns drawing members of your family and extended family at the table below. As each family member draws a person at the table, tell a story about why this person is important to your family and to your beliefs. When all the family members are drawn in, remember that whenever you gather in his name, Jesus is always there with you.

Visit **www.ChristOurLife.org/family** for more family resources.

Special Seasons and Lessons

The Year in Our Church

Advent

Christmas

Ordinary Time

Lent

Holy Week

Christmas

Epiphany

Ash Wednesday

Easter Sunday

Easter

First Sunday of Advent

Feast of All Saints

Winter

Spring

Fall

Summer

Pentecost

Ordinary Time

Liturgical Calendar

The liturgical calendar highlights the feast days and seasons of the Church year. Various colors symbolize the different seasons.

1 | Feast of All Saints

We Celebrate the Feast of All Saints

Who is in your family? Some families are huge. Others are small. Grandparents are part of our family. Aunts, uncles, and cousins are part of our family too. Each person is unique. We share a special love for our family.

We belong to another family. This family is called the Communion of Saints. It is a very large family. The Communion of Saints is the family of the Church. This family cares for and helps one another on the journey to God.

The saints are part of this family who live with God in heaven. These saints pray for us. They show us how to live as Christ's disciples.

Each member of the Communion of Saints is unique. Christ's love bonds us all together.

On November 1, we celebrate All Saints Day. We honor all of the saints on this day. We remember our large family of faith. We ask the saints to help us. We pray that we will one day be with God and the saints in heaven.

Saint Cecilia

Saint Patrick

Saint Francis of Assisi

Called to Be Saints

Mark the pictures that show we are on the way to becoming saints.

Get Baptized

Pray Often

Love God by Serving Others

Ask the Saints to Pray for Us

Seek God's Forgiveness

Forgive Others

2 | Advent

John the Baptist Was Chosen by God

Print the baby's name on the line:

_____

- - - - - - - - - - - -

_____

John

Zechariah's Song

You, child, will be called prophet of the Most High,

for you will go before the Lord to prepare his ways.

(adapted from Luke 1:76)

God sent John the Baptist. God knew John would help prepare the way for Jesus. John would lead the people down a straight path to God.

A person chosen by God to speak God's message is called a prophet. John the Baptist is a prophet. During Advent we remember the message of John the Baptist. We prepare the way for Jesus. We make a straight path to God.

We Prepare for Jesus

Write how you will prepare for Jesus during Advent.

3 | Christmas

A Christmas Play

Reader 1: A long time ago, God our Father promised a Savior. For many years, the Jewish people waited for the Savior to come. Then, one day, God fulfilled his promise. He sent us his only Son, Jesus. We remember this event as the first Christmas.

Choir: (*sings "O Come, O Come, Emmanuel"*)

Reader 2: God chose a young woman named Mary to be the Mother of his Son. Mary lived in a little village called Nazareth. She loved God very much and always said yes to him. God sent one of his angels to ask Mary to be the Mother of the Savior. The angel's name was Gabriel. The angel came to Mary and said:

Gabriel: Hail Mary, full of grace, the Lord is with you. Do not be afraid. God is pleased with you. You will have a baby. You must name him Jesus. He will be holy and will be called the Son of God. He will be the Savior of the world. Your relative Elizabeth, who is old, will have a baby too, for God can do all things.

Mary: I am the servant of the Lord. I accept God's plan for me.

Choir: (*sings or says "Hail Mary"*)

Reader 3: One day, Joseph brought home news that they must travel to Bethlehem in order to be counted. Mary and Joseph packed the things they needed. Joseph got the donkey ready. Soon, they were on their way. Mary rode the donkey and Joseph walked. They traveled many days over the rocky roads. Finally, they reached Bethlehem.

Choir: (sings "O Little Town of Bethlehem")

Reader 4: Mary and Joseph went from place to place looking for a room but could find none. Finally, a man told Joseph that in the hillside there was a cave, which had once been a stable. When they got there, they found that it was small but quiet. Mary and Joseph thanked the good man. They settled in and rested from their journey. That night, while everything was still, Jesus, the Son of God, was born.

Choir: (sings "Silent Night")

Reader 5: In the countryside nearby, there were shepherds in the fields. They took turns watching the flocks of sheep during the night. An angel of the Lord appeared to them and the glory of the Lord shone around them. The shepherds were afraid, but the angel said:

Angel: Do not be afraid. Listen, for I bring you news of great joy. Today, in the town of Bethlehem, a Savior has been born to you. He is Christ the Lord. You will find him wrapped in swaddling clothes and lying in a manger.

Shepherds: Let us go to Bethlehem and see this newborn Savior!

Choir: (sings "Hark! The Herald Angels Sing")

Reader 6: Let us give Jesus the gift of our heart.

4 | Lent

A Time of Sacrifice

Lent is a special time to show Jesus, our Savior, how much we love him. We remember that Jesus died on the cross. Jesus made this sacrifice for us. We make sacrifices to thank Jesus for his love.

A sacrifice is a gift we give to God to give him thanks. When we make a sacrifice, we give up something important. We make a sacrifice when we give up playtime in order to help someone. We make a sacrifice when we eat food we do not like without complaining.

When we make a sacrifice for Jesus, we can pray,

"All for you, O Jesus."

What sacrifices can you make during Lent?

Sacrifices for Jesus

Fill in the words that are missing in these sentences.

Word Bank

~~TV~~   ~~OK~~

~~work~~   ~~snack~~

We can share our favorite ___snack___ with someone.

We can do our best ___work___ in school.

We can help someone instead of watching ___Tv___ .

We can say ___OK___ when we cannot have what we want.

I will make this sacrifice to thank Jesus for his sacrifice on the cross:

_____ .

5 | Holy Week

The Holiest Week of the Year

The week before Easter is called Holy Week.
It is the holiest week of the year. We prepare to celebrate Jesus'
Resurrection at Easter. There are many special days during
Holy Week.

Palm (Passion) Sunday

At church on Palm, or Passion, Sunday, palm branches are
blessed. We process with them. We hear the Gospel about
Jesus' death on the cross. After Mass we put the blessed palms
in our homes. They remind us that we want to love and praise
Jesus every day.

Holy Thursday

At church on Holy Thursday, we remember Jesus' Last Supper
and how Jesus washed his disciples' feet. Jesus gave us a
special gift at the Last Supper. He offered us the gift of his
Body and Blood in the Eucharist.

Good Friday

After the Last Supper, Jesus went into a garden to pray. There he was arrested and taken to prison. On Good Friday morning Jesus was brought before Pilate, the ruler, who sentenced him to die on the cross. The soldiers made Jesus carry a rough, heavy cross to the top of a hill called Calvary. There they nailed him on the cross. After three hours Jesus bowed his head and died.

Holy Saturday

On Holy Saturday we remember that Jesus was buried in the tomb. We wait in hope and, after sundown, people go to church to celebrate the Resurrection.

Match the day of Holy Week with the event.

Palm Sunday	Holy Thursday	Good Friday

6 | Easter

Easter is a season of joy. We celebrate the good news that Jesus has risen from the dead. We pray, "Alleluia! Alleluia!"

The Story of Easter

Mary Magdalene and the other Mary came to the tomb where Jesus had been buried.

There they saw an angel who rolled back the stone that had covered the tomb. The angel sat on the stone and spoke to the women. He said, "Do not be afraid. You are looking for Jesus. He is not here. He has been raised just as he said. Come, and see the place where he was buried. Then go and tell his disciples."

The women ran to tell the news to the disciples.

(adapted from Matthew 28:1–8)

Like the women, we share our Easter joy with others.

Easter Prayer

Reader 1: After Jesus died on Good Friday, his body was wrapped in cloth and laid in a tomb. Soldiers guarded the tomb so that no one would take Jesus' body. But Jesus rose from the dead. This is what we celebrate at Easter.

Leader: Think of Jesus' love for us. He gave his life for us so that we could live forever in heaven. Let's thank Jesus for his love. *(Pause for silent prayer.)*

Reader 2: *(Read Matthew 28:1–8)*

Song

Offering

Leader: After each reading, we respond "Alleluia! Alleluia!"

Reader 3: Jesus rose from the dead on Easter Sunday morning with a new and glorious life . . .

Reader 4: Jesus shared his risen life with his Mother and friends . . .

Reader 5: He shares his life with us . . .

Reader 6: We can live and love like Jesus . . .

Reader 7: We can live forever with Jesus . . .

Leader: Jesus did so much for us when he died and rose from the dead. He gave us a share in his life. He gives us light to help us see the way to heaven.

Song

7 | Pentecost

We Receive the Holy Spirit

Jesus promised to send his disciples the gift of the Holy Spirit. On Pentecost, the Holy Spirit came to the disciples. The Holy Spirit helped them to understand everything that Jesus had taught them. They told everyone the good news of Jesus. They showed people God's love.

On Pentecost Sunday, we celebrate the gift of the Holy Spirit. The word *Pentecost* means "fifty." We celebrate Pentecost fifty days after Easter.

At our Baptism, we received the gift of the Holy Spirit. What are some things the Holy Spirit helps us to do?

We pray to the Holy Spirit:

Give us   Fill our hearts with

___ ___ ___ ___ ___   ___ ___ ___ ___
5   2   4   1   3   5   6   8   7

H	I	T	G	L	O	E	V
1	2	3	4	5	6	7	8

Pentecost Prayer

Reader 1: A reading from the Gospel of John.

On the evening before he died, Jesus promised to send the Holy Spirit to his disciples. He said, "I will send you the Holy Spirit. He will come to you from my Father and will help you understand all about me. He will help you and guide you. Then you must tell everyone about me. You must be a light for all people."

(adapted from John 15:26–27)

Leader: Let us pray that the Holy Spirit will help us and guide us, so that we can tell others how good Jesus is. After each prayer our response is: "Help us and guide us."

All: Help us and guide us.

Reader 2: A reading from the Acts of the Apostles.

On Pentecost, Mary and all the apostles came together to pray. Suddenly there was a sound like a strong wind blowing. Then something that looked like flames of fire could be seen above the heads of each one. They were all filled with the Holy Spirit. They were all filled with love for Jesus. Peter and the other apostles went out and told everyone about Jesus.

(adapted from Acts of the Apostles 2:1–4,14)

Leader: The Holy Spirit will give us more love if we ask. After each prayer our response is: "Fill our hearts with love."

All: Fill our hearts with love.

Leader: Let us pray together our prayers to the Holy Spirit.

All: Holy Spirit, help us and guide us.
Holy Spirit, fill our hearts with love. Amen.

8 | The Missions

God Loves Everyone in the World

God our heavenly Father made everyone in this world. He loves each and every person. Because God is our Father, everyone he made is our sister or brother.

God wants us to take care of one another. We do this by being kind and helping others. We can also take care of one another by making sure that everyone knows how much God loves them. The Church calls people who work to spread this good news *missionaries*.

Saint Thérèse Shows Us How to Be Missionaries

Saint Thérèse was a missionary in the Church, although she never left her convent. Ever since Thérèse was a young girl, she wanted to spread the good news about Jesus. She wanted to go to faraway countries to tell people who had never heard about Jesus. But God wanted her to be a missionary at home. How did she do this?

Saint Thérèse prayed and made sacrifices for people all over the world right from her own home.

We too can be missionaries and spread God's love by our prayers and sacrifices.

We can ask Saint Thérèse to help us ask God to bless all people.

We Remember

Whom does Jesus love?
Jesus loves everyone in the world.

We Respond

Holy Mary, pray for us and for all the children of the world.

What Catholics Should Know

(continued on next page)

(continued from page 163)

Prayer and How We Pray

Prayer is talking and listening to God. We can talk to God in the words of special prayers or in our own words. We can pray out loud or silently. We can pray to God often and in many different ways. We can praise God. We can ask him for what we need and thank him. We can pray for ourselves and for others. (See the inside front and back covers of your book for the prayers we use most often.)

Additional Catholic Prayers

It is good for us to know prayers by heart. To learn prayers by heart means that we not only learn, or memorize, the words, but try to understand and live them.

Apostles' Creed

I believe in God, the Father almighty,
      creator of heaven and earth.
I believe in Jesus Christ, his only Son, our Lord.
         He was conceived by the power of the Holy Spirit
               and born of the Virgin Mary.
         He suffered under Pontius Pilate,
               was crucified, died, and was buried.
         He descended to the dead.
         On the third day he arose again.
         He ascended into heaven,
               and is seated at the right hand of the Father.
         He will come again to judge the living and the dead.
I believe in the Holy Spirit,
         the holy catholic Church,
         the communion of saints,
         the forgiveness of sins,
         the resurrection of the body,
         and the life everlasting. Amen.

Hail, Holy Queen

Hail, holy Queen, Mother of mercy,
hail, our life, our sweetness, and our hope.
To you we cry, the children of Eve;
to you we send up our sighs,
mourning and weeping in this land of exile.
Turn, then, most gracious advocate,
your eyes of mercy toward us;
lead us home at last
and show us the blessed fruit of your womb, Jesus:
O clement, O loving, O sweet Virgin Mary.

Prayer for Vocations

God, thank you for loving me.
You have called me
to live as your child.
Help all your children
to love you and one another.
Amen.

Pope Benedict XVI has suggested that certain prayers that are shared by the universal Church could be learned in Latin and prayed as a sign of the universal nature of the Church. English versions of the following prayers appear on the inside front cover.

Signum Crucis
(Sign of the Cross)

In nomine Patris,
et Filii,
et Spiritus Sancti.
Amen.

Gloria Patri
(Glory Be to the Father)

Gloria Patri,
et Filio,
et Spiritui Sancto.
Sicut erat in principio,
et nunc, et semper,
Et in saecula saeculorum.
Amen.

Pater Noster
(Our Father)

Pater noster, qui es in caelis,
sanctificetur nomen tuum.
Adveniat regnum tuum.
Fiat voluntas tua,
sicut in caelo et in terra.
Panem nostrum quotidianum da nobis hodie,
et dimitte nobis debita nostra
sicut et nos dimittimus debitoribus nostris.
Et ne nos inducas in tentationem,
sed libera nos a malo.
Amen.

Ave Maria
(Hail Mary)

Ave Maria, gratia plena,
Dominus tecum.
Benedicta tu in mulieribus,
et benedictus fructus ventris tui, Iesus.
Sancta Maria, Mater Dei, ora pro nobis peccatoribus,
nunc, et in hora mortis nostrae.
Amen.

The Rosary

The Rosary helps us remember the special events, or mysteries, in the lives of Jesus and Mary. We begin by praying the Sign of the Cross while holding the crucifix. Then we pray the Apostles' Creed.

We pray the Our Father as we hold the first single bead. On each of the next three beads, we pray a Hail Mary. Next, we pray a Glory Be to the Father. On the next single bead, we think about the first mystery, a particular event in the lives of Jesus and Mary. We then pray the Our Father.

Each of the 5 sets of 10 beads is called a decade. As we pray each decade, we reflect on a different mystery. Between the sets is a single bead on which we think about one of the mysteries and pray the Our Father. We then pray a Hail Mary as we hold each of the beads in the set. At the end of each set, we pray a Glory Be to the Father. In some places people pray the Hail, Holy Queen after the last decade. See page 167. We end by holding the crucifix as we pray the Sign of the Cross.

PRAYING THE ROSARY

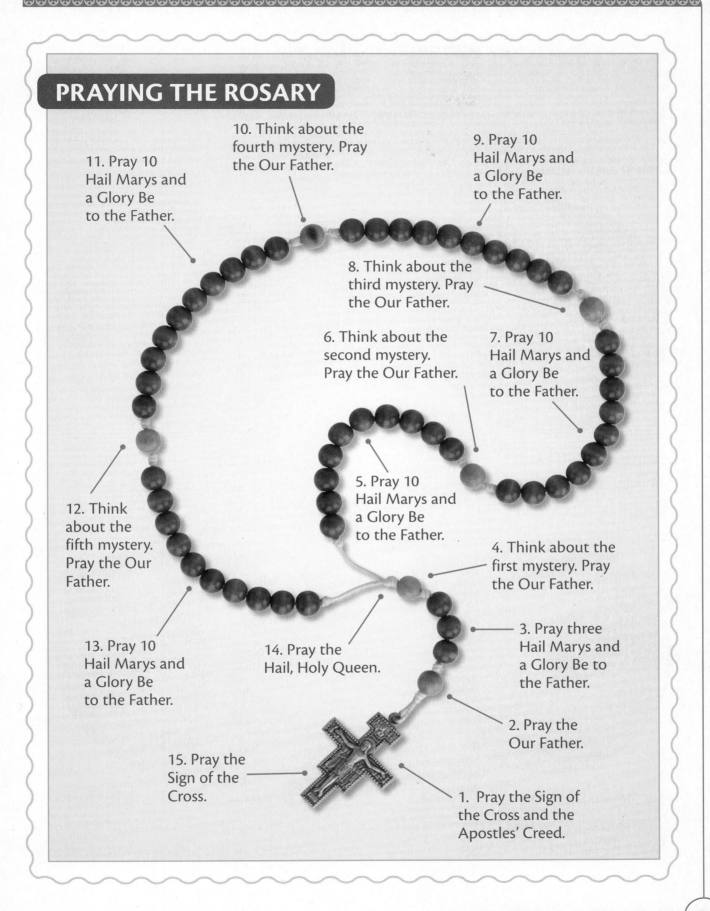

10. Think about the fourth mystery. Pray the Our Father.

11. Pray 10 Hail Marys and a Glory Be to the Father.

9. Pray 10 Hail Marys and a Glory Be to the Father.

8. Think about the third mystery. Pray the Our Father.

6. Think about the second mystery. Pray the Our Father.

7. Pray 10 Hail Marys and a Glory Be to the Father.

5. Pray 10 Hail Marys and a Glory Be to the Father.

12. Think about the fifth mystery. Pray the Our Father.

4. Think about the first mystery. Pray the Our Father.

13. Pray 10 Hail Marys and a Glory Be to the Father.

14. Pray the Hail, Holy Queen.

3. Pray three Hail Marys and a Glory Be to the Father.

2. Pray the Our Father.

15. Pray the Sign of the Cross.

1. Pray the Sign of the Cross and the Apostles' Creed.

Stations of the Cross

The 14 Stations of the Cross represent events from Jesus' passion and death. At each station we use our senses and our imagination to remember Jesus' suffering, death, and Resurrection.

Jesus Must Die
Pontius Pilate sentences Jesus to death.

Jesus Takes His Cross
Jesus accepts his cross.

Jesus Falls
Weakened by his suffering, Jesus falls beneath the cross.

Jesus Meets His Mother
Jesus meets his Mother, Mary, who is sad to see Jesus suffer.

Simon Helps Jesus
Soldiers force Simon to carry
the cross.

Veronica Helps Jesus
Veronica steps through
the crowd to wipe the face
of Jesus.

Jesus Falls the Second Time
Jesus falls under the weight of
the cross a second time.

The Women
Are Sorry for Jesus
Jesus tells the women
not to cry for him.

Jesus Falls Again
Jesus falls a third time.

Jesus' Clothes Are Taken Away
The soldiers take away Jesus'
clothes. They hurt him.

Jesus Is Nailed to the Cross
Jesus' hands and feet are
nailed to the cross.

Jesus Dies on the Cross

After three hours on the cross, Jesus bows his head and dies.

Jesus Is Taken Down

Mary holds Jesus in her arms.

Jesus Is Buried

Jesus' disciples place his body in the tomb.

The closing prayer—sometimes included as the 15th station—reflects on the Resurrection of Jesus.

The Seven Sacraments

The sacraments are signs of the grace we receive from God. Sacraments show that God is part of our lives. They were given to the Church by Jesus to show that he loves us. The seven sacraments help us live the way God wants us to live. The sacraments are celebrated with us by priests.

Baptism

Baptism is the first sacrament we receive. Through Baptism, we become followers of Jesus and part of God's family, the Church. The pouring of water is the main sign of Baptism. Along with Confirmation and the Eucharist, Baptism is a Sacrament of Initiation.

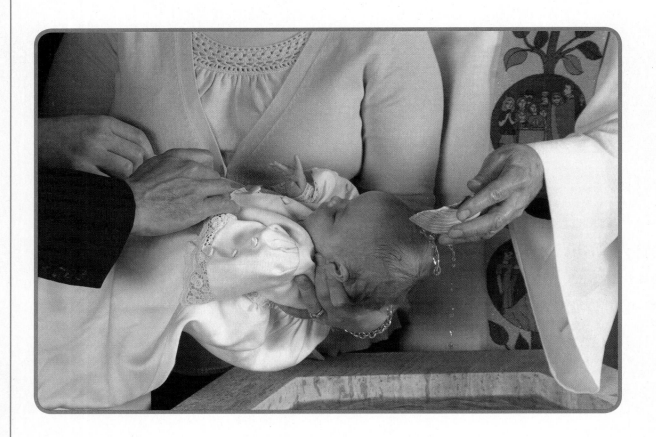

Confirmation

Confirmation is a Sacrament of Initiation. In this sacrament, the Holy Spirit strengthens us to be witnesses to Jesus. Confirmation makes us stronger in faith and helps us become better Christians. The bishop places holy oil in the form of a cross on our foreheads. This is the main sign of Confirmation.

The Eucharist

The Eucharist is a Sacrament of Initiation. At Mass, the bread and wine become the Body and Blood of Jesus Christ. This happens when the priest says the words of consecration that Jesus used at the Last Supper. The Eucharist is also called Holy Communion.

Penance and Reconciliation

We ask God to forgive our sins in the Sacrament of Penance and Reconciliation. The priest who celebrates this sacrament with us shares Jesus' gifts of peace and forgiveness. God always forgives us when we are sorry and do penance for our sins.

Anointing of the Sick

In this sacrament, a sick person is anointed with holy oil and receives the healing of Jesus.

Holy Orders

Some men are called to be deacons, priests, or bishops. They receive the Sacrament of Holy Orders. Through Holy Orders, the mission, or task, given by Jesus to his apostles continues in the Church.

Matrimony

Some men and women are called to be married. In the Sacrament of Matrimony, they make a solemn promise to be partners for life, both for their own good and for the good of the children they will raise.

Holy Days of Obligation

Holy Days of Obligation are the days other than Sundays on which Catholics are required to gather for Mass to celebrate the great things God has done for us through Jesus and the saints.

Six Holy Days of Obligation are celebrated in the United States.

January 1—Mary, Mother of God

40 days after Easter—Ascension (in many U.S. dioceses, the Seventh Sunday of Easter)

August 15— Assumption of the Blessed Virgin Mary

November 1—All Saints

December 8—Immaculate Conception

December 25—Nativity of Our Lord Jesus Christ

Commandments

The Ten Commandments

God gave us the Ten Commandments. They teach us how to live for God and for others. They help us follow the moral law to do good and avoid evil.

1. I am your God; love no one or anything more than me.
2. Use God's name with respect.
3. Keep the Lord's day holy.
4. Honor and obey your parents.
5. Treat all human life with respect.
6. Respect your body and the bodies of others.
7. Respect what belongs to others.
8. Tell the truth.
9. In marriage, husbands and wives respect each other.
10. Be happy with what you have.

The Great Commandment

People asked Jesus, "What is the most important commandment?" Jesus said, "First, love God. Love him with your heart, soul, and mind. The second is like it: Love your neighbor as much as you love yourself." (adapted from Matthew 22:37–39) We call this the Great Commandment.

The New Commandment

Before his death on the cross, Jesus gave his disciples a new commandment: "Love one another. As I have loved you, so you also should love one another." (adapted from John 13:34)

Making Good Choices

The Holy Spirit helps us make good choices. We get help from the Ten Commandments, the grace of the sacraments, and the teachings of the Church. We also get help from the example of the saints and fellow Christians. To make good choices, we should ask ourselves the following questions:

1. Is the thing I am choosing to do a good thing?
2. Am I choosing to do it for the right reasons?
3. Am I choosing to do it at the right time and in the right place?

The Bible

God speaks to us in many ways. One way is through the Bible. The Bible is the story of God's promise to care for us, especially through his Son, Jesus. The Bible is made up of two parts. The Old Testament tells stories about God and the Jewish people before Jesus was born. In the New Testament, Jesus teaches us about the Father's love. The Gospels tell stories about Jesus' life, death, and Resurrection. At Mass, we hear stories from the Bible. We can also read the Bible on our own.

Showing Our Love for the World

Jesus taught us to care for those in need. The social teachings of the Church call us to follow Jesus' example in each of the following areas:

Life and Dignity
God wants us to care for everyone. We are all made in God's image.

Family and Community
Jesus wants us to be loving helpers in our families and communities.

Rights and Responsibilities
All people should have what they need to live good lives.

The Poor and Vulnerable
Jesus calls us to do what we can to help people in need.

Work and Workers
The work that we do gives glory to God.

Solidarity
Since God is our Father, we are called to treat everyone in the world as brothers and sisters.

God's Creation
We show our love for God's world by taking care of it.

Glossary

A

absolution the forgiveness of God. In the Sacrament of Penance and Reconciliation, we say that we are sorry for our sins. Then the priest offers us God's absolution.

altar the table in the church on which the priest celebrates Mass

ambo a platform from which a person reads the Word of God during Mass

angel a messenger from God

apostle one of twelve special men who followed Jesus and saw him after the Resurrection. These were the people sent to preach the Gospel to the whole world.

B

Baptism the first of the three sacraments by which we become members of the Church. Baptism frees us from original sin and gives us new life in Jesus Christ through the Holy Spirit.

Baptism

Bible the written story of God's promise to care for us, especially through his Son, Jesus

bishop a leader in the Church. Bishops teach us what God is asking of us as followers of Jesus today.

Blessed Sacrament the Body of Christ. It is kept in the tabernacle to be adored and to be taken to the sick and the dying.

Body and Blood of Christ the bread and wine consecrated by the priest at Mass

C

catholic a word that means "all over the world." The Church is catholic because Jesus gave the Church to the whole world.

Christ a title, like *Messiah*, that means "anointed with oil." This name is given to Jesus after the Resurrection.

Christian the name given to people who want to live as Jesus taught us to live

Christmas the day on which we celebrate the birth of Jesus

Christmas

Church the name given to the followers of Christ all over the world. Spelled with a small *c*, the church is the building where we gather to pray to God.

commandment a rule that tells us how to live as God wants us to live

confession the act of telling our sins to a priest in the Sacrament of Penance and Reconciliation

Confirmation the sacrament that completes the grace we receive in Baptism

contrition the sadness we feel when we know that we have sinned

creation everything that God has made. God said that all creation is good.

Creator God, who made everything that is

Easter

D

deacon a man who accepts God's call to serve the Church. Deacons help the bishop and priests in the work of the Church.

disciple a person who is a follower of Jesus and tries to live as he did

E

Easter the celebration of the raising of Jesus Christ from the dead. Easter is the most important Christian feast.

Emmanuel a name that means "God with us." It is a name given to Jesus.

disciple

Eucharist the sacrament in which we give thanks to God for giving us Jesus Christ. We receive the Body and Blood of Jesus Christ at Mass.

The Gospel is read at Mass.

F

faith a gift of God. Faith helps us believe in God and live as he wants us to live.

G

Gospel the good news of God's love for us. We learn this news in the story of Jesus' life, death, and Resurrection. The story is presented to us in the Gospels of Matthew, Mark, Luke, and John.

grace the gift of God given to us without our earning it. Sanctifying grace fills us with God's life and makes us his friends.

Great Commandment Jesus' important teaching that we are to love both God and other people

H

heaven the life with God that is full of happiness and never ends

holy describing the kind of life we live when we cooperate with the grace of God

Holy Communion the Body and Blood of Jesus Christ that we receive

Holy Family the family made up of Jesus; his mother, Mary; and his foster father, Joseph

Holy Spirit the third Person of the Trinity, who comes to us in Baptism and fills us with God's life

J

Jesus the Son of God, who was born of the Virgin Mary, died, was raised from the dead, and saves us so that we can live with God forever

Holy Communion

Joseph the foster father of Jesus, who was engaged to Mary when the angel announced that Mary would have a child through the power of the Holy Spirit

L

Last Supper the last meal Jesus ate with his disciples on the night before he died. Every Mass is a remembrance of that last meal.

Lord's Day Sunday, the day on which Jesus rose from the dead. It is a special day for Christians to worship God.

Joseph and Jesus

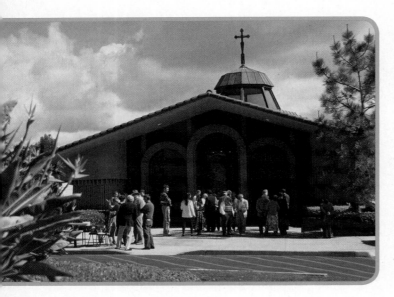

parish

M

Mary the mother of Jesus. She is called "full of grace" because God chose her to be Jesus' mother.

Mass our most important means of praying to God. At Mass we listen to God's Word, the Bible. We receive the Body and Blood of Jesus Christ in Holy Communion.

miracle acts of wonder that cannot be explained by natural causes. They are works of God. In the Gospels, Jesus works miracles as a sign that God is present in his ministry.

N

New Testament the story of Jesus and the early Church

O

Old Testament the story of God's plan for the salvation of all people

original sin the result of the sin of Adam and Eve. They disobeyed God and chose to follow their own will rather than God's will.

P

parish a community of believers in Jesus Christ who meet regularly to worship God together

Passover the Jewish festival that commemorates the delivery of God's people from slavery in Egypt. In the Eucharist we celebrate our passover from death to life through Jesus' death and Resurrection.

penance the turning away from sin because we want to live as God wants us to live (*See* Sacrament of Penance and Reconciliation.)

pope the bishop of Rome, successor of Saint Peter, and leader of the Roman Catholic Church

prayer the raising of our hearts and minds to God. We are able to speak to and listen to God in prayer because he teaches us how to do so.

priest a man who accepts God's special call to serve the Church. Priests guide the Church and lead it in the celebration of the sacraments.

R

reconciliation making friends again after a friendship has been broken by some action or lack of action. In the Sacrament of Penance and Reconciliation, we are reconciled with God, the Church, and others.

Resurrection the bodily raising of Jesus Christ from the dead on the third day after he died on the cross

S

sacrament the way in which God enters our life. Through simple objects such as water, oil, and bread, Jesus continues to bless us.

Sacrament of Penance and Reconciliation the sacrament in which we celebrate God's forgiveness of our sins when we say to the priest that we are sorry for them

sacrifice a gift given to God to give him thanks. Jesus' death on the cross was the greatest sacrifice.

saint a holy person who died as a true friend of God and now lives with God forever

Savior Jesus, the Son of God, who became human to make us friends with God again. The name *Jesus* means "God saves."

Savior

sin a choice to do what is wrong on purpose. A sin is when you say no to God.

T

tabernacle the container in which the Blessed Sacrament is kept so that Holy Communion can be taken to the sick and the dying

temptation a thought or feeling that can lead us to disobey God. Temptation can come either from outside us or inside us.

Ten Commandments the 10 rules that God gave to Moses. The Ten Commandments sum up God's law and show us how to live as his children.

Trinity the mystery of one God, existing in three Persons: the Father, the Son, and the Holy Spirit

Index

neighbor as yourself
    (*see* Commandment, Great)
Luke (Gospel), 102

M

Mark (Gospel), 102
Martha, 77
Mary, 77, 190
    Christmas, 151–52
    holding Jesus' body after he dies, 175
    Mother of the Church, 11, 136, 138
    sadness at Son's suffering, 172
    wedding at Cana, 135
Mary Magdalene, 157
Mass, 190
    bread, 107, 110
    confession, general, 97
    gathering, 96
    gifts, 107, 110, 112
    Jesus' sacrifice, 92
    order of, 100, 106, 110, 114, 120
    readings, 106
    rituals, 34
    Sunday, 31
    wine, 107, 110
    Word of God, 105, 106
Matrimony, Sacrament of, 179
Matthew (Gospel), 102
Matthew, Saint, 49
mezuzah, 50b
miracles, 190
    loaves and fish, 85
missionaries, 131, 161, 162
Moses, 50b

N

New Testament, 22, 190
Nicene Creed, 103
Noah, 126d

O

obedience
    Jesus', 37
    to God, 37, 59
Old Testament, 22, 190
original sin, 15, 26a, 190
Our Father, 137, 169. *See also* Lord's Prayer

P

Palm Sunday, 155
parish, 190
Passion Sunday, 155
Passover, 89, 90, 190
Pater Noster, 169. *See also* Our Father
Paul VI, Pope, 144c

peace of the Lord, 61, 64, 115, 121
penance, 70, 75, 190. *See also* Penance
    and Reconciliation
Penance and Reconciliation, Sacrament
    of, 61, 178, 191
    absolution (*see* absolution)
    confessing sins, 70
    contrition (*see* contrition)
    family, receiving together, 82a, 82b, 82d
    priest's role, 70, 74, 75
Pentecost, 159, 160
Peter, Saint, 35
phylactery, 50b
Pontius Pilate, 172
pope, 190
    Holy Father, 130
    leader of Church, 18
prayer, 191. *See also* prayers
    daily, 32, 34
    grace before meals, 40
Prayer for Vocations, 167
prayers. *See also* prayer
    Apostles' Creed, 26c, 166
    Easter, 158
    Eucharistic, 111
    Glory Be to the Father, 137, 142, 168, 170
    Hail, Holy Queen, 167
    Hail Mary 137, 138, 169
    Our Father 137, 169. *See also* Lord's Prayer
    Pentecost, 160
    Prayer for Vocations, 167
    Rosary, 137, 170, 171
    talking to God, 165
priests, 130, 191
puzzle, Church, 23

R

reconciliation, 191. *See also* forgiveness; Penance
    and Reconciliation
repentance, 54
Resurrection, 155, 175, 191
Rosary, 137, 170, 171

S

Sacraments, 176–79, 191
    Anointing of the Sick (*see* Anointing of the Sick)
    Baptism (*see* Baptism)
    Confirmation (*see* Confirmation)
    definition, 15
    Eucharist (*see* Eucharist)
    Holy Orders (*see* Holy Orders)
    Matrimony (*see* Matrimony)
    Penance and Reconciliation
        (*see* Penance and Reconciliation)
sacrifice of Jesus, 112, 153
sacrifices, 153, 191

definition, 48
Jesus' (*see* sacrifice of Jesus)
Thérèse, Saint, example of, 46
saints, 144c, 191. *See also* specific saints
calling, 148
definition, 22
Savior, 10, 191
selfishness, 54
Sign of the Cross, 13, 14, 26c, 168
Baptism, during, 16
Rosary, as part of praying the, 170
Sacrament of Penance and
Reconciliation, use during, 75
Signum Crucis, 168. *See also* Sign of the Cross
Simon, Saint, 173
sin, 192
definition, 64
forgiving (*see* forgiveness)
original (*see* original sin)
sisters, 131
social teachings of Church, 184
songs as a form of praise, 34
Stations of the Cross, 172–75

T

tabernacle, 50a, 122, 192
temptation, 60, 192
Ten Commandments. *See* Commandments, Ten
Thérèse, Saint, 45, 46, 162
Trinity, 4, 192
definition, 8
Trinity Sunday, 126c

V

Veronica, 173

Z

Zacchaeus, 55, 56, 58, 82d
Zechariah, 149

Scripture Index

OLD TESTAMENT

Deuteronomy
6:6–9, p. 50b

Psalms
40:6, p. 8
51:1–14, pp. 73, 81
51:12, p. 76
118:1, p. 76
139:1–5, p. 32
139:14, p. 1, 4

NEW TESTAMENT

Matthew
5:14–16, p. 82d
5:24, p. 72
8:5–13, p. 116
9:9, p. 49
22:37–39, p. 181
25:35, p. 105
25:35–36, p. 36

25:35–40, p. 40
28:1–8, p. 157

Mark
2:5, p. 70
7:31–37, p. 21
12:30, pp. 30, 35
12:31, p. 35
14:22–24, p. 125

Luke
1:42, p. 138
1:76, p. 149
7:36–50, p. 62
12:24–29, p. 6
18:16, p. 95
19:5, p. 58
22:19, pp. 94, 95

John
2:1–11, p. 135
6:35, p. 85
6:51, pp. 83, 86, 88,
120, 142
8:12, p. 70
10:14,16, p. 130
12:24, p.10

13:14–15, p. 90
13:34, pp. 90, 181
14:6, p. 14
14:16, p. 65
14:26, pp. 65, 68
14:27, pp. 51, 115
14:31, p. 37
15:5–7, pp. 12, 14, 25
15:10–11, p. 29
15:12, p. 48
15:14, pp. 53, 58
15:26–27, p. 160
19:25–27, p. 136
20:19, p. 64
20:19–23, p. 61

Acts of the Apostles
2:1–4,14, p. 160

Romans
12:9–18, p. 44

1 Corinthians
11:23–25, p. 91
12:13, pp. 127, 129
13:4–6, p. 134

2 Corinthians
9:7, p. 105

Ephesians
2:19, p. 19
4:5,11–16, p. 143
5:18–19, p. 34
6:1, p. 105

1 John
3:1, p. 15
4:9, p. 20
4:16, pp. 27, 44

Art Credits

When there is more than one picture on a page, credits are supplied in sequence, left to right, top to bottom. Page positions are abbreviated as follows: (t) top, (c) center, (b) bottom, (l) left, (r) right.

FRONT MATTER:
iii(t) © The Crosiers/Gene Plaisted OSC
iv(tr) © The Crosiers/Gene Plaisted OSC

UNIT 1:
1 Getty/Amana Images/Camelot
2(t,b) Getty/Camelot
4(b) © The Crosiers/Gene Plaisted OSC
5(t) Len Ebert
6 Sally Schaedler
9(t) Sally Schaedler
10(t) © The Crosiers/Gene Plaisted OSC
10(b) Laser Type and Graphics
11 Sally Schaedler
12(r) Jack Jasper
13 Phil Martin Photography
15–18 Phil Martin Photography
19 Sally Schaedler
21(c,b) Laser Type and Graphics
22(t) © Cleo Freelance Photography
22(bl,br) © The Crosiers/Gene Plaisted OSC
23 Laser Type and Graphics
24 Len Ebert
26d Phil Martin Photography

UNIT 2:
27–28 Andreanna Seymore/Stone/Getty
29(b) © The Crosiers/Gene Plaisted OSC
30 Sally Schaedler
31(t) Phil Martin Photography
32–33 Laser Type and Graphics
35(b) Sally Schaedler
36(c) © Myrleen Ferguson Cate/PhotoEdit, Inc.
36(br) © Myrlene Fergusen/Photoedit
37(t) Len Ebert
39 Tom Foty
42(b) Mel Yates/Stone/Getty
44 Laser Type and Graphics
45(t) Katja Zimmermann/Taxi/Getty
45 © Office Central de Lisieux
47 Laser Type and Graphics
49–50 © The Crosiers/Gene Plaisted OSC
50a © Jonathon Nourack/Photoedit
50b © Ilan Rosen/Alamy
50c(b) Ava Russell

UNIT 2:
51–52 Phil Martin Photography
53(b) © The Crosiers/Gene Plaisted OSC
54 Phil Martin Photography
55 Don Dyen
60 Len Ebert
61(t) Sally Schaedler
62 Sally Schaedler
63 Larry Frederick/John Walter & Associates

65(b) © The Crosiers/Gene Plaisted OSC
70 © The Crosiers/Gene Plaisted OSC
73(b) © Christie's Images/SuperStock, Inc.
74 Phil Martin Photography
75 Len Ebert
76(r) Diane Johnson
77(b) Sally Schaedler
78 Don Dyen
80–82 © The Crosiers/Gene Plaisted OSC
82b–82c(bl) George Hamblin/Steven Edsey & Sons

UNIT 4:
83–84 © The Crosiers/Gene Plaisted OSC
85(b) © The Crosiers/Gene Plaisted OSC
86 Sally Schaedler
89(t) © Bill Aron/PhotoEdit, Inc.
89(cl,cr,bl,br) Don Dyen
90(tr) Sally Schaedler
91 © The Crosiers/Gene Plaisted OSC
92(tl) © W.P. Wittman Limited
92(tr) © The Crosiers/Gene Plaisted OSC
93 Proof Positive/Farrowlyne Assoc., Inc.
94 Len Ebert
95(t) © Mike Goldwater/Alamy
95(b) © The Crosiers/Gene Plaisted OSC
97 © Myrleen Ferguson Cate/PhotoEdit, Inc.
100 Len Ebert
101(t) © The Crosiers/Gene Plaisted OSC
102 Diane Johnson
103 © The Crosiers/Gene Plaisted OSC
104(tr) © Cleo Freelance Photography
104(b) Digital Stock
105 Len Ebert
107(t) © World Religions Photo Library/Alamy
109(b)–110 Diane Johnson
111(t) Tony Freeman/PhotoEdit, Inc.
111(b) © The Crosiers/Gene Plaisted OSC
114 Len Ebert
115(t) Phil Martin Photography
115(b) © The Crosiers/Gene Plaisted OSC
116 Sally Schaedler
118–119(b) W. P. Wittman Limited
121(b) © The Crosiers/Gene Plaisted OSC
122 Len Ebert
123(br) Marla Sweeney/Taxi/Getty
123(cr) © Photo Network/Alamy
123(br) Marla Sweeney/Taxi/Getty
125–126 © The Crosiers/Gene Plaisted OSC
126a(b) © Andrew Parker/Alamy
126b(b) © WoodyStock/Alamy
126c(l) © Titus/Getty

UNIT 5:
127–128 © VATICAN POOL/epa/Corbis
130(tr) © The Crosiers/Gene Plaisted OSC
131(t,c) Pavel Chichikov/Ponkawonka
132–133 Len Ebert
134 Laser Type and Graphics
135(t) © Van Hilversum/Alamy

135(b) Sally Schaedler
136 © The Crosiers/Gene Plaisted OSC
139(b) Laser Type and Graphics
140 Diane Johnson
143-144 © The Crosiers/Gene Plaisted OSC
144b(l) © The Crosiers/Gene Plaisted OSC
144(c) © Bettmann/Corbis

SPECIAL SEASONS AND LESSONS:
145(t) © The Crosiers/Gene Plaisted OSC
146 Susan Tolonen
147 © The Crosiers/Gene Plaisted OSC
148 Nan Brooks
149 Don Dyen
153 © The Crosiers/Gene Plaisted OSC
154t Sally Schaedler
155(b) © The Crosiers/Gene Plaisted OSC
156(t) © The Crosiers/Gene Plaisted OSC
157(t) © The Crosiers/Gene Plaisted OSC
158 © The Crosiers/Gene Plaisted OSC
162(t) Don Dyen

WHAT CATHOLICS SHOULD KNOW:
168 © Vatican Pool/Corbis
169(t) © The Crosiers/Gene Plaisted OSC
171 Greg Kuepfer
172–175 © The Crosiers/Gene Plaisted OSC
176 Phil Martin Photography
177(t) Phil Martin Photography
177(c) © Myrleen Ferguson Cate/PhotoEdit
178(t) © Myrleen Ferguson Cate/PhotoEdit
178(b) © Alan Oddie/PhotoEdit
180 © Tony Freeman/PhotoEdit

GLOSSARY:
188(t) Phil Martin Photography
191 © The Crosiers/Gene Plaisted OSC

LESSON PULLOUTS:
199(bl,br) Diana Bush
200 Phyllis Pollema-Cahill
First Communion Booklet: Ralph Smith
Scripture Prayer Booklet, 1: © The Crosiers/Gene Plaisted OSC
Scripture Prayer Booklet, 2: Laser Type and Graphics
Scripture Prayer Booklet, 12: Diane Johnson
Punchouts,1-2: Diana Bush
Punchouts,3-4: Len Ebert

Lesson Pullouts

- **First Communion Pullouts**

- **Manger Figures**

- **Christmas Songs**

- **Easter Eggs/Basket**

- **Scripture Prayer Booklet "I am the Good Shepherd"**

- **Punchouts**

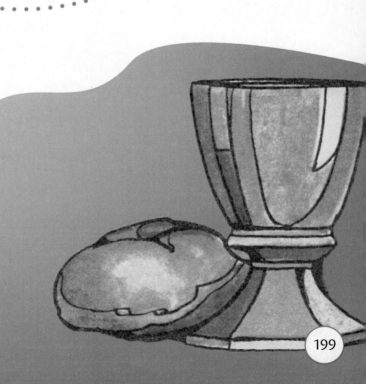

Let the children come to me for the kingdom of heaven belongs to them.

adapted from Matthew 19:14

You are invited.

Fold

Dear _____,

You are invited to prepare to receive Jesus in Holy Communion.

God's people would like you to join them at the table of the Lord.

You will be enrolled at a special celebration to be held at _____

on _____ at _____ o'clock.

Please come.

Please sign the form and return it to your teacher to let me know if you will be here.

In Christ,

_____

Dear Father _____,

I am happy to be a Catholic Christian.

I would like to prepare to receive Jesus in Holy Communion.

I will try to prepare well.

I will be at the celebration.

_____

- -

_____

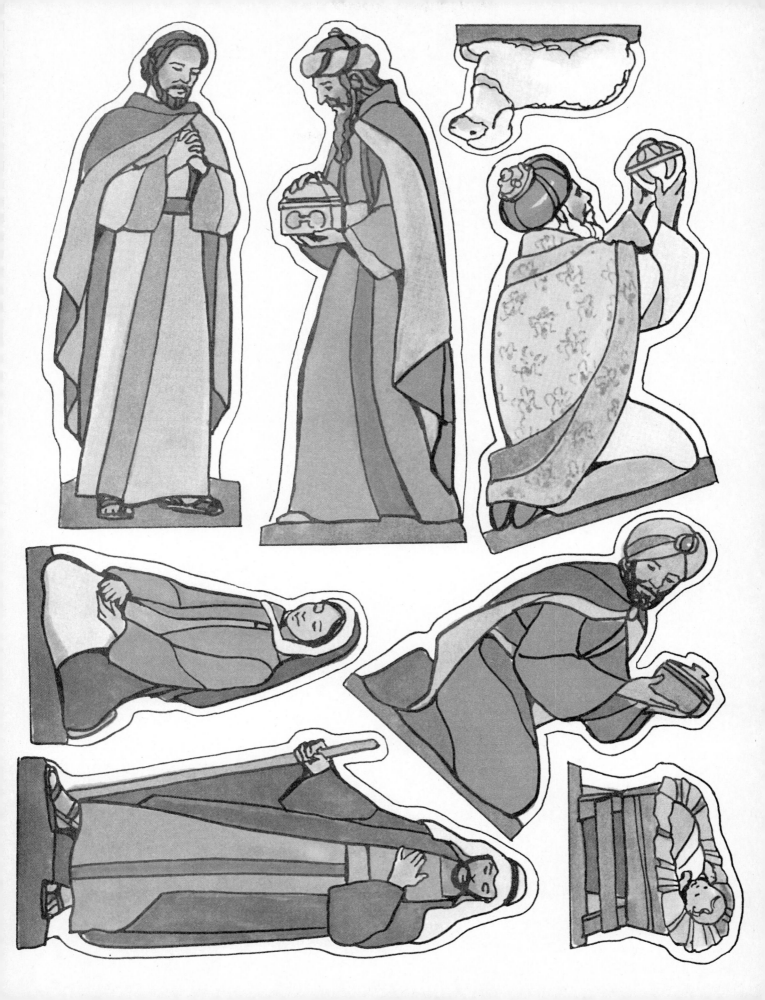

O Little Town of Bethlehem

by Phillips Brooks

O little town of Bethlehem,
How still we see thee lie!
Above thy deep and dreamless sleep
The silent stars go by.
Yet in thy dark streets shineth
The everlasting Light;
The hopes and fears of all the years
Are met in thee tonight.

O holy Child of Bethlehem,
Descend to us we pray.
Cast out our sin and enter in;
Be born in us today.
We hear the Christmas angels
The great glad tidings tell;
O, come to us, abide with us,
Our Lord Emmanuel!

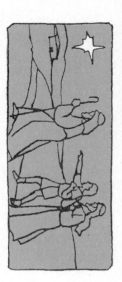

O Come, O Come, Emmanuel

O come, O come, Emmanuel,
And ransom captive Israel
That mourns in lonely exile here
Until the Son of God appear.
Rejoice! Rejoice! O Israel,
To you shall come Emmanuel.

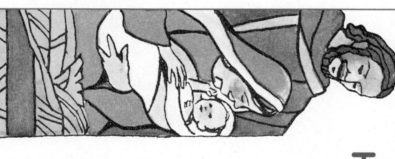

Hail Mary

Hail Mary, full of grace!
the Lord is with you;
blessed are you among
women,
and blessed is the fruit
of your womb, Jesus.
Holy Mary, Mother of God,
pray for us sinners,
now and at the hour of our
death.

Amen.

Hark, the Herald Angels Sing

Hark, the herald angels sing,
"Glory to the newborn King;
Peace on earth, and mercy mild,
God and sinners reconciled."
Joyful all ye nations rise,
Join the triumph of the skies.
With angelic hosts proclaim,
"Christ is born in Bethlehem."
Hark, the herald angels sing,
"Glory to the newborn King."

Silent Night

Franz Grüber, Joseph Mohr

Silent night, holy night.
All is calm, all is bright.
'Round yon Virgin Mother and Child.
Holy infant, so tender and mild.
Sleep in heavenly peace,
Sleep in heavenly peace.

Silent night, holy night.
Shepherds quake at the sight.
Glories stream from heaven afar.
Heavenly hosts sing Alleluia.
Christ, the Savior, is born!
Christ, the Savior, is born!

Make an Easter Basket of Love for Jesus

- Use an egg cup from an egg carton.

- Glue on a piece of ribbon for a handle.

- Cut out or have someone else help you cut out the eggs and place them in an envelope.

- Put the basket in your room.

- Each morning after you pray, take an egg from the envelope and read it. Place it in front of your basket.

- Make the sacrifice during the day to show love for Jesus.

- After your night prayers, put the egg in the basket. If you forget to make the sacrifice, put the egg back in the envelope.

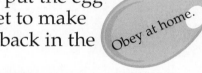

Do the dishes.

Clean your room.

Be kind today.

Obey at home.

Set the table.

Clean your room.

Dust the house.

Thank Jesus for dying on the cross.

Help someone today.

Say something kind to someone.

Say the Our Father for the poor.

Obey at home.

Do the dishes.

Make someone happy today.

Do the dishes.

Eat all your food at mealtime.

Show someone you care about him or her.

Help around the house.

Give in to others.

Tell Jesus you love him.

Do not watch TV today.

Thank your parents for what they do.

Set the table.

Do not eat candy.

Make someone happy.

Say a prayer for the sick.

Clean your room.

Pick up things from the floor.

Do the dishes.

Share something today

Do neat work in school.

Tell your parents you love them today.

Tell your parents you love them.

Obey in school.

Dust the house.

Pick up your toys.

Dust the house.

Say something kind to someone.

Play with someone who looks lonely

Smile at someone.

Be kind today

Do not watch TV today.

Be kind to someone.

Give up candy or snacks today.

Do you want to be a lamb in Jesus' flock?

**Read the verses here.
Ask Jesus to help you
live them.**

Blessed are the peacemakers.
Mt 5:9

Come to me.
Mt 11:28

Children, obey your parents.
Eph 6:1

Do to others whatever you would have them do to you.
Mt 7:12

Love is kind.
1 Cor 13:4

Do not worry.
Mt 6:25

Scripture Prayer Booklet

I am the
Good Shepherd

John 10:11

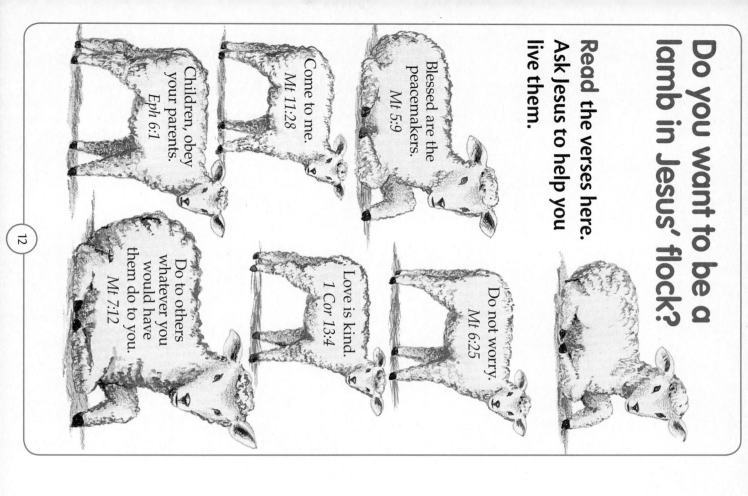

This book belongs to
_____

Words from the Bible that help me pray . . . .

Write some Bible verses on the rungs.

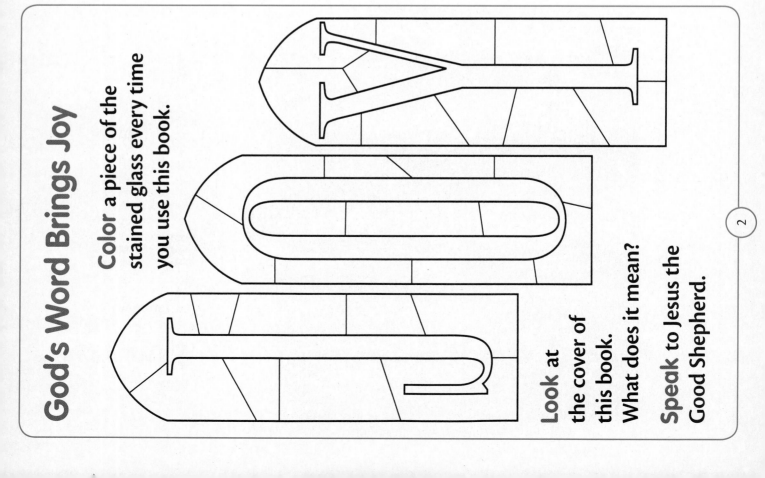

God's Word Brings Joy

Color a piece of the stained glass every time you use this book.

Look at the cover of this book. What does it mean?

Speak to Jesus the Good Shepherd.

Favorite Bible Stories

Draw a picture for each story.
Add your favorite story.

Jesus Cures Someone	Jesus at Sea
Jesus Rises	

Thank Jesus for something he did.

Flowers to pray from . . . .

Do not be afraid.
Mk 5:36

Love one another.
Jn 13:34

Be quiet.
Lk 4:35

Keep my commandments.
Jn 14:15

Pray to your Father.
Mt 6:6

Prayers from the Mass

Do this in memory of me.

Lk 22:19

Blessed be God.

Lord, have mercy.

Thanks be to God.

Praise to you, Lord Jesus Christ.

Glory to you, Lord.

Alleluia.

Lift up your hearts.

Let us give thanks.

Lord, I am not worthy.

Go in peace.

You are the light of the world.

Mt 5:14

Write inside the big star the names of people you want to pray for. Color a small star when you pray for one of them.

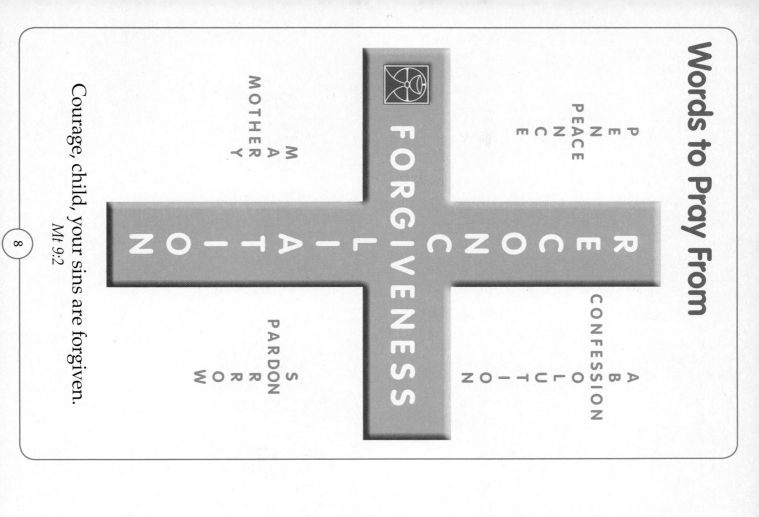

Words to Pray From

P
E
N
A
PEACE
N
C
E

A
B
CONFESSION
O
L
U
T
I
O
N

FORGIVENESS

RECONCILIATION

M
MOTHER
A
R
Y

S
PARDON
R
R
O
W

Courage, child, your sins are forgiven.
Mt 9:2

8

O Jesus, I am sorry for the times . . .

I talked back to someone.

I pouted.

I did not play fair.

I got into a fight.

I gave someone a hard time.

I was noisy.

I was annoying on purpose.

I hurt others' feelings.

I was stubborn.

I was selfish.

I did not listen to you, Lord.

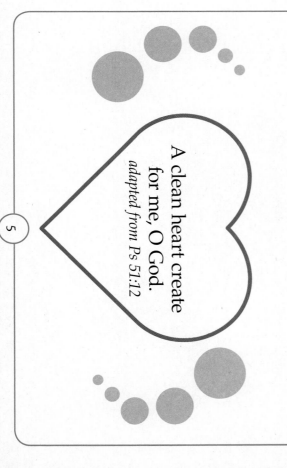

A clean heart create
for me, O God.
adapted from Ps 51:12

5

God cares for us . . .

You are the God who works wonders.

adapted from Ps 77:15

God indeed is my savior.

Is 12:2

I put my trust in you.

Ps 55:24

The Lord gives wisdom.

Prv 2:5

You are safe.

Tb 12:17

Be happy.

Tb 8:21

The Lord himself gives all good things.

Tb 4:19

Be grateful to the Lord.

Jdt 8:25

You, Lord, help and comfort me.

Ps 86:17

The Lord gives health and life and blessing.

Sir 34:17

Your hands made me.

Ps 119:73

O God, you have not left those who love you.

adapted from Dn 14:38

The eyes of the Lord watch all things.

adapted from Prv 15:3

The Lord heard their cry.

Jdt 4:13

You are before me and behind me.

adapted from Ps 139:5

I myself will care for my sheep.

adapted from Ez 34:15

Think about it.

Fold

My Morning Offering

God, our Father, I offer you today
all I think and do and say.
I offer it with what was done on
earth by Jesus Christ, your Son.

Fold
Back

it
produces
much
fruit.

adapted from
John 12:24

If
a
seed
dies,

Fold
Back

Chapter 16

Chapter 2

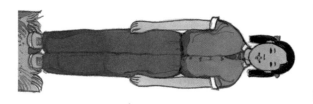

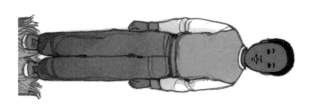

Chapter 7

Cover design by

Chapter 5

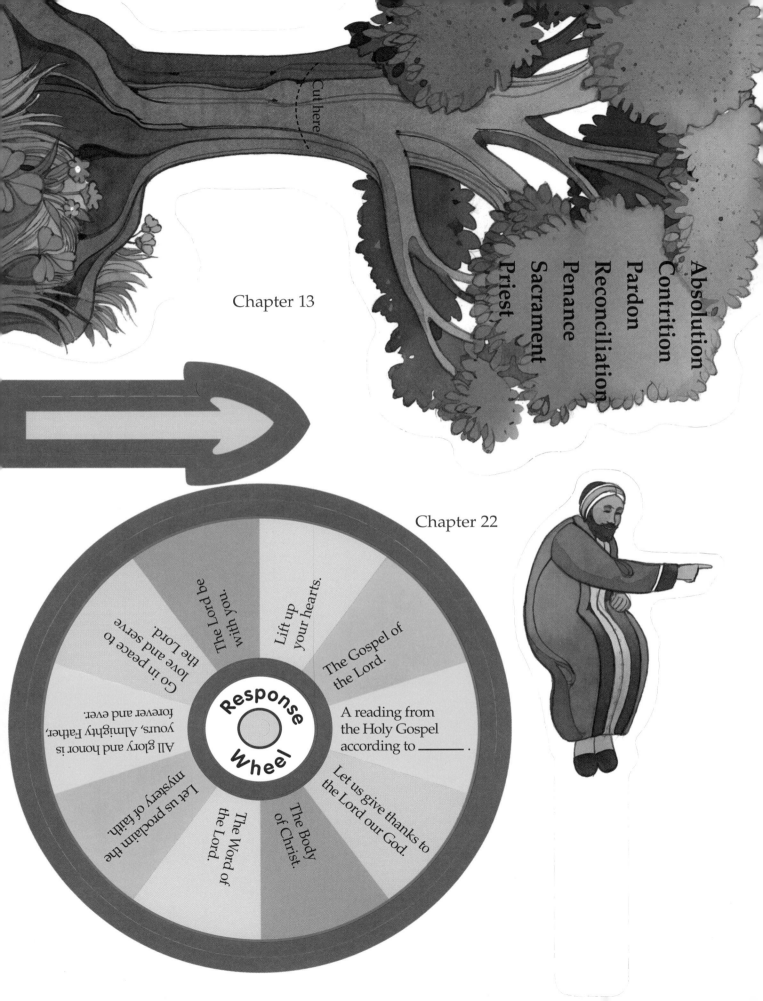

Chapter 13

Absolution
Contrition
Pardon
Reconciliation
Penance
Sacrament
Priest

Cut here

Chapter 22

Response Wheel

The Lord be with you.

Lift up your hearts.

The Gospel of the Lord.

A reading from the Holy Gospel according to _____.

Let us give thanks to the Lord our God.

The Body of Christ.

The Word of the Lord.

Let us proclaim the mystery of faith.

All glory and honor is yours, Almighty Father, forever and ever.

Go in peace to love and serve the Lord.